SPALDING.

BASEBALL

CROSSWORDS

Mark Roszkowski

MP
MASTERS PRESS

A Division of Howard W. Sams & Co.

Published by Masters Press (A Division of Howard W. Sams)
2647 Waterfront Pkwy E. Dr., Suite 300
Indianapolis, IN 46214

Library of Congress Cataloging-in-Publication Data

Roszkowsi, Mark.
  Spalding baseball crosswords / Mark Roszkowski.
    p. cm. — (Spalding sports library)
  ISBN 00-940279-55-X : $9.95
    1. Baseball—United States—Clubs—History.
    2. Baseball—United States—History. 3. Crossword puzzles.
    I. Title. II. Series.
GV875.A1R67 1993   92-42411
796.357'64--dc20   CIP

Credits:

  Cover design: Michelle Holden

  Cover photo provided by the Cleveland Indians.

TABLE OF CONTENTS

To my wonderful wife, Sue.

FOREWORD

In baseball, few things are as precious for spanning the game's history as the stories that are shared and passed from one generation to the next. These stories of players' heroics, owners' exploits, fans' enthusiasm, and teams' collapses are the very fabric upon which baseball tradition is built.

In no other sport is the history of a franchise or the exploits of its players more well documented, preserved, and expanded upon than in the grand old game of baseball. This is the beauty of baseball: Passing along the legends of the sport and the players is the very essence of the game.

These stories keep the players alive for one generation of fans after another. The greats of years past serve as yardsticks for measuring the exploits of the modern heroes of the game. This means that Babe Ruth is almost as relevant to the game today as he was more than half a century ago. As are Honus Wagner, Ted Williams, and Hank Aaron.

The yardsticks for measuring excellence, or lack thereof, are abundant in baseball. No other sport enjoys such an elaborate universe of statistics to measure a player's performance.

With batting averages, earned run averages, runs batted in, men left on base, hits with men on third base and less than two out, inherited runners stranded on base, and many others, baseball has more statistics than the Toronto Blue Jays have fans in the Sky Dome.

All of these statistics are useful. Depending upon your degree of interest, you can choose any and all parts of the stats to make sense out of what your favorite team or player is doing.

Years ago when I covered the Detroit Tigers as a beat writer for *The Detroit News* , I had to carry a variety of record books for quick statistical reference and comparison to meet story deadlines. Today, with the advent of computerization, there is an onslaught of player and team statistical breakdowns. There are more numbers available for instantaneous use than Abner Doubleday and the other early publishers of baseball statistics could have ever dreamed of.

With all of the enthusiasm for information available on the sport of baseball, the histories, the legends, the statistics, I can only be amazed that there hasn't been a book like this before. A book that combines all the elements that people love about baseball with a fun twist to see how much they know (or can guess) about America's pastime.

Mark Roszkowski, a lifetime enthusiast of the sport, has done a masterful job compiling the basic team histories and highlighting them with relevant numbers as well as statistical information of the past ten years. He has added fun to learning about the various teams by creating the crossword puzzles on each team.

The puzzles are challenging and focus only on the team's history. There are no "filler" questions. If you get stuck, reach for a baseball encyclopedia or reference book (before you look up the answer in the back of the book!). The more you learn, the more you will appreciate this sport and its rich stock of characters and legends.

A nostalgic, informative, and fun-filled book about baseball, I recommend *Baseball Crosswords* to fans of all degrees. So grab your pencil and step up to the plate, here's a whole new way to enjoy your favorite sport.

Dan Ewald
Public Relations Director
The Detroit Tigers

BALTIMORE ORIOLES

Baltimore's rich baseball history dates back to the heyday of the old Orioles of the National League in the 1890's. The team was famous for its fierce, hard nosed and tactically brilliant style of play. It featured future Hall of Famers John McGraw at third base, Willie Keeler in right, Joe Kelley in left, and Hughie Jennings at short.

Baltimore was left out when the National League shook down to eight teams in 1890. A Baltimore team was included in the new American League in 1901, but it lasted only two seasons before moving to New York to become the Highlanders (later the Yankees). It wasn't until 1954 that Baltimore again hosted a major league baseball team.

Baseball returned to Baltimore in the form of the former St. Louis Browns. The Browns sparkled but a few times in their history.

Up until the 1920's, neither the Browns nor the other St. Louis team, the Cardinals, had won a pennant. Around that time, both teams came up with a franchise player to try and lift their fortunes. For the Cards, it was Rogers Hornsby. For the Browns, it was George Sisler.

In 1922, the Browns just missed the pennant, losing by one game to Babe Ruth's Yankees. Sisler had a remarkable year, batting a torrid .422. He was aided by a strong supporting cast of Ken Williams, Jack Tobin, Baby Doll Jacobson, and Urban Shocker. The Browns did not challenge again for two decades.

During World War II, many of baseball's best players were called into military service. Rather than encourage the teams to stop playing, President Roosevelt urged the major leagues to continue their schedules as a diversion for the American people from the war.

The war-time teams had to fill their positions with men who were either too young, too old, or medically unfit to fight. This situation favored the Browns, who lost fewer players to the war than any other team, and, in 1944, the Browns capitalized by winning their first American League pennant. The World Series that year pitted the Browns against the Cardinals, an all-St. Louis Series. The Cards

1

won in six games. This one and only World Series appearance is the highlight of Browns' history.

In 1954, the team moved to Baltimore and a slow, methodical rebuilding process began. However, there were some high points during this time, for example Hoyt Wilhelm's 1958 no-hitter against the Yankees and Jim Gentile's five grand slams in 1961 (two in one game).

Manager Paul Richards assembled a tough young pitching staff in the early sixties. The Baby Birds, as they were known, included Wally Bunker, Chuck Estrada, Jack Fisher, Jerry Walker, and Milt Pappas. Around this same time, third baseman Brooks Robinson, who joined the team in the mid-fifties, blossomed into one of the AL's biggest stars. In 1964, the flashy third baseman won the AL MVP award. Brooks was an integral part of the Baltimore championships teams that would follow.

The acquisition of Frank Robinson in 1965 from the Cincinnati Reds put the O's over the top, and 1966 marked the franchise's first world championship. Frank won the triple crown his first year in the American League, and the Orioles stunned Sandy Koufax, Don Drysdale and the Dodgers in a four-game World Series sweep.

The Birds took the pennant again in 1969 but were stunned themselves in the World Series that year by the Miracle Mets. The Orioles recovered and beat the Reds to win the World Championship in 1970. Brooks Robinson's spectacular plays at third in this series will not soon be forgotten. The O's won the AL East three more times in this period, in 1971, 1973, and 1974.

The Orioles took the AL crown again in 1979, led by the Cy Young performance of Mike Flanagan and the hitting of the veteran Ken Singleton and a young Eddie Murray. Baltimore had a three-games-to-one lead in the World Series but wound up losing to Willie Stargell and the Pirates.

Earl Weaver retired as manager in 1982 after fifteen years, and his replacement, Joe Altobelli led the O's to a world championship in his first try. American League MVP Cal Ripken provided leadership on the field and Murray provided great offensive stats (33 HR, 111 RBI, .308 BA) as Baltimore defeated the Phillies 4-1 in the Series.

In 1992, the new Baltimore stadium, Oriole Park at Camden Yards, became the showplace of baseball. Renewed fan interest helped inspire a strong showing by the ballclub. The Orioles remained in the pennant race until the last two weeks of the season. Oriole Park will be a perfect setting for Baltimore fans to watch newly signed Cal Ripken attempt to break Lou Gehrig's record of 2,130 consecutive games.

Division Finishes 1983-1992

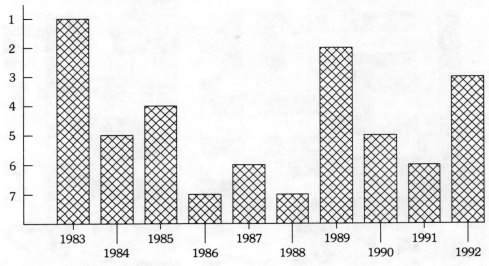

League Leaders 1983-1992

Category	Year	Leader	
MVP	1983	Cal Ripken	
Doubles		Cal Ripken	47
Runs		Cal Ripken	121
Hits		Cal Ripken	211
ERA	1984	Mike Boddicker	2.79
Wins		Mike Boddicker	20
Rookie of the Year	1989	Gregg Olson	
MVP	1991	Cal Ripken	

1992 Leaders

Category	Player	
Batting Average	Mike Devereaux	.276
Home Runs	Mike Devereaux	24
RBI	Mike Devereaux	107
Stolen Bases	Brady Anderson	53
Doubles	Cal Ripken	29 (T)
	Mike Devereaux	29 (T)
Triples	Mike Devereaux	11
Runs	Brady Anderson	100
Hits	Mike Devereaux	180
Wins	Mike Mussina	18
ERA	Mike Mussina	2.54
Strikeouts	Ben McDonald	158
Saves	Gregg Olson	36

Solution on page 136.

ACROSS

1. This Hall of Famer batted .420 for the Browns in 1922, George _____ .

3. This Oriole outfielder was named Rookie of the Year in 1973, Al _____ .

5. Switch hitting outfielder for the 1983 World Champion Orioles, John _____ .

9. He won 18 games as an Oriole rookie in 1960, Chuck _____ .

11. He shut out the Dodgers 1-0 in the final game of the 1966 World Series, Dave _____ .

12. Shortstop for the 1979 AL champions, Kiko _____ .

13. Catcher for the 1970 World Champion Orioles, _____ Hendricks

15. Left fielder for the world champs in 1970, Don _____ .

16. Baltimore's Gold Glove shortstop of the seventies, Mark _____ .

17. Led the Orioles with 16 saves in 1969, Eddie _____ .

20. He managed the Orioles to a title in 1966, _____ Bauer.

22. Great Browns pitcher who won 27 games in 1921, Urban _____ .

23. American League triple crown winner in 1966.

27. Orioles manager from 1955 to 1961, Paul _____ .

28. He was one of four 20 game winners for the Birds in 1971, right-hander Pat _____ .

30. He became baseball's first 30-30 man for the Browns in 1922, Ken _____ .

33. Manager of Oriole pennant winners in 1969, 1970, 1971, and 1979, Earl _____ .

34. This bullpen ace has collected 131 saves for the Birds through 1992, Gregg _____ .

35. Catcher for the 1966 World Champion Oriole team, Andy _____ .

36. Second baseman on the 1979 AL champion Oriole club, Rich _____ .

DOWN

1. Hitting star of the 1944 AL Champion Browns with 20 homers and 109 RBI, Vern _____ .

2. He was named Rookie of the Year in 1949 as an outfielder for the Browns, Roy _____ .

3. Centerfielder on several pennant-winning Oriole teams in the 60's and 70's, Paul _____ .

4. Oriole first baseman from 1989 to 1992, Randy _____ .

6. He had a 10-5 record in relief for the 1970 Champion Birds, Dick _____ .

7. This right-hander won 13 and lost 13 for the 1992 Orioles (two words).

8. This legendary pitcher hurled for the hapless Browns in the early fifties, Satchel _____ .

10. He won 20 games for the O's in 1980, Scott _____ .

14. One of the pitching stars of the 1966 World Series, Moe _____ .

18. Oriole catcher from the fifties, Gus _____ .

19. Browns owner in the early fifties, Bill _____ .

21. As a rookie in 1983, he posted a 16-8 record for the World Champion Orioles, Mike _____ .

24. This Hall of Famer played shortstop for the Browns from 1902 to 1916, Bobby _____ .

25. Baltimore catcher who belted 20 homers in 1992, Chris _____ .

26. Centerfielder for the St. Louis Browns in the twenties, Baby _____ Jacobson.

29. Oriole pitching ace who entered the Hall of Fame in 1990.

31. The Orioles' leadoff hitter who hit 21 homers and knocked in 80 in 1992, _____ Anderson.

32. He was the American League MVP in 1970, _____ Powell.

BOSTON RED SOX

T he United States was at war in the summer of 1918. Many baseball players left the diamond to fight in Europe. Back home in Boston, one of the players called to serve was Red Sox leftfielder Duffy Lewis. To replace him, Boston manager Ed Barrow decided to place one of his pitchers in the outfield between starts. The pitcher responded that year with a 13-7 record but shocked everyone by leading the league in home runs. His name was Babe Ruth.

The Sox took the World Series that year in what had become a fall routine for them. In the fifteen World Series played to that point, the Sox had participated in five of them and won them all, making them baseball's most successful team at that time.

In 1903, the Boston club, then called the Pilgrims, defeated the Pittsburgh Pirates in the very first World Series. The victory elevated the newly formed American League to a par even with the older, established National League. This defeat stung the senior circuit so badly that they refused to re-stage the World Series the following year.

Another great Red Sox championship came in 1912. Boston defeated the New York Giants in a dramatic World Series. In the final game, the Sox came to bat in the bottom of the tenth inning trailing by a run and facing the great Christy Mathewson on the mound. A couple of Giant miscues and some clutch Boston hitting gave the championship to the Red Sox, thrilling the home town fans in their brand new stadium, Fenway Park.

This era of greatness ended in 1919, when Red Sox owner Harry Frazee responded to his unraveling finances by selling off his star players to raise the money to pay his debts. The death knell occurred in 1920, when Frazee sold the emerging superstar Ruth to the Yankees for $100,000. At this moment, the fortunes of these two teams were reversed. The Yankees, unsuccessful to that point, began a dynasty unparalleled in American sports, while the Red Sox entered an era of frustration, never again to taste champagne from the victory cup.

The Red Sox fortunes brightened in 1939 when owner Tom Yawkey brought a rookie outfielder named Ted Williams to Boston. Williams electrified fans with his hitting talents. Yawkey had brought other big name talents to Boston, Lefty Grove, Jimmie Foxx, and Joe Cronin, all Hall of Famers, but none of these stars had the success or the popularity that Williams did.

Williams is considered the greatest natural hitter of all time. His lifetime marks include 521 career home runs, a total cut far short of what it potentially could have been, because Williams served five years in the military during the prime of his career. Williams finished with a career .344 batting average and 1,839 RBIs.

In 1946, Williams and the rest of baseball's soldiers returned to the game, and the Red Sox won the American League pennant in convincing fashion with a twelve game margin over the second place Tigers. However, they also began their new tradition of postseason near misses, losing the World Series in seven games to the St. Louis Cardinals as Enos Slaughter made his famous "mad dash" to home in the eighth inning of the final game scoring the deciding run.

The near misses continued in 1948 and 1949. In 1948, the Red Sox and the Cleveland Indians finished the season in a tie. The Tribe took a one-game playoff to decide the pennant and went on to take the World Series. In 1949, the Red Sox lost the last two games of the season to the Yankees and the pennant by one game. This is the closest they would get to the top for eighteen years.

When the 1967 season started, nobody expected anything great from the Bosox, who by now had become second division fixtures. However, new manager Dick Williams had other ideas. Under his leadership (and aided by a triple crown season from Carl Yastrzemski, a Cy Young pitching performance by Jim Lonborg, and a brilliant mid-season acquisition of outfielder Ken Harrelson and catcher Elston Howard.) the Sox shocked the baseball world by winning a tight four-team pennant race on the last day of the season.

Even though they lost the World Series in seven games to the Cardinals, the '67 season marked a distinct change in Red Sox fortunes as they changed overnight into perennial pennant contenders and remained among baseball's elite teams throughout the seventies and eighties.

The postseason near misses have continued. Neither Carlton Fisk, Louis Tiant nor Rookie phenom Fred Lynn could pull the Sox ahead of the Reds in the 1975 Series, but they came as close as can be imagined. The Sox faltered again in 1978, blowing a big division lead, then losing to Bucky Dent and the Yankeees in a one game division-deciding playoff.

In the eighties, the Sox developed two of the games's biggest stars, Roger Clemens and Wade Boggs. Clemens "the Rocket" has completely dominated AL batters. Already in his young career, Clemens has won three Cy Young Awards and an MVP award in 1986. Boggs was the most prolific hitter of the eighties, winning batting titles in five of his first six full seasons. These two led the Red Sox into the 1986 Series against the Mets. They watched a championship they should have won pass them by when Mookie Wilson's grounder went through Bill Buckner's legs.

Solution on page 136.

ACROSS

4. The team was known as the Boston _____ when they won the first-ever World Series in 1903.

7. This Hall of Famer played third for Boston in the early 1900's, Jimmy _____ .

8. This DiMaggio spent his career with the Red Sox.

9. Dan Shaughnessy's book, *The Curse of the* _____ .

11. Bill Lee.

16. Boston's biggest power threat in 1992, rightfielder Tom _____ .

17. The Rocket.

18. Centerfielder for the 1967 AL champs, _____ Smith.

20. He won the 1950 AL batting title as a utility player for the Sox, Billy _____ .

21. Acquired from the Angels, this second baseman was the team's best base stealer in the early 80's, Jerry _____ .

23. He went 21-13 for the 1918 World Champion Red Sox and added two World Series wins, Carl _____ .

25. First baseman who missed the 1992 season due to injury, Carlos _____ .

28. Catcher signed by the Red Sox as a free agent in 1989, Tony _____ .

29. Known as the Golden Greek, his untimely death at age 25 in 1955 shocked Boston fans, Harry _____ .

30. Red Sox infielder drafted by the Colorado Rockies, then traded to the Dodgers, Jody _____ .

31. Shortstop for the 1967 club, and third baseman for the 1975 pennant winners, _____ Petrocelli.

33. He notched a league-leading 31 saves for the Sox in 1977, Bill _____ .

36. Strikeout (abbrev.).

37. The _____ Splinter.

38. Hall of Fame Red Sox owner, Tom _____ .

39. He led the Bosox to the 1975 pennant while winning both the Rookie of the Year and MVP awards.

40. This second baseman led all hitters in the 1986 World Series with a .433 average, Marty _____ .

41. Had a great rookie year in 1980, hitting .321, stayed with the Red Sox through '86, Dave _____ .

DOWN

1. Hall of Fame Red Sox rightfielder from 1909 to 1920, Harry _____ .

2. He pitched a scoreless twelfth and picked up the victory in the unforgettable Game 6 of the 1975 World Series, Rick _____ .

3. He won 20 games three times for Boston in the 1970's.

5. The ace of the pitching staff for the 1967 AL champs, Jim _____ .

6. Hard throwing reliever Dick Radatz was known by this name.

8. He was thrown out at the plate by George Foster in the bottom of the ninth of Game 6, 1975 World Series, sending the game into extra innings, Denny _____ .

10. Shortstop for the 1975 AL champs, Rick _____ .

12. Led the AL with 32 homers in 1965, Tony _____ .

13. He pitched a no-hitter against the White Sox in 1962, Bill _____ .

14. American League MVP in 1978.

15. He played short and batted .335 for the 1946 pennant-winning Red Sox, Johnny _____ .

19. This lefty ace won 25 games for the Red Sox in 1949 (two words).

22. Had a great year for the Sox in 1989, (30 HR, 117 RBI) but has suffered from health problems ever since, Nick _____ .

24. This bullpen workhorse logged a record 168 innings pitched in relief in 1982, Bob _____ .

26. This slugger had a career year for the Sox in 1984, leading the league in HR and RBI, Tony _____ .

27. Home of the Red Sox, _____ Park.

32. This left-hander was traded to the Pirates after the 1983 season for Mike Easler, John _____ .

34. This Bosox lefty went 14-3 in 1975, Roger _____ .

35. 1992 marked the first time this third baseman ever batted under .300.

Division Finishes 1983-1992

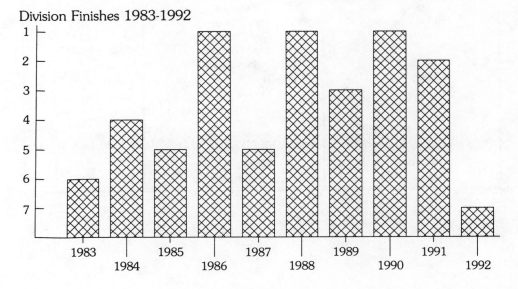

League Leaders 1983-1992

Category	Year	Leader	
Batting Average	1983	Wade Boggs	.361
Home Runs		Jim Rice	39
Home Runs	1984	Tony Armas	43
RBI		Tony Armas	123
Runs		Dwight Evans	121
Batting Average	1985	Wade Boggs	.368
Hits		Wade Boggs	240
MVP	1986	Roger Clemens	
Cy Young		Roger Clemens	
Batting Average		Wade Boggs	.357
ERA		Roger Clemens	2.48
Wins		Roger Clemens	24
Winning Pct.		Roger Clemens	.857(24-4)
Cy Young	1987	Roger Clemens	
Batting Average		Wade Boggs	.363
Wins		Roger Clemens	20 (T)
Winning Pct.		Roger Clemens	.690 (20-9)
Batting Average	1988	Wade Boggs	.366
Strikeouts		Roger Clemens	291
Doubles		Wade Boggs	45
Runs		Wade Boggs	128
Doubles	1989	Wade Boggs	51
Runs		Wade Boggs	113 (T)
ERA	1990	Roger Clemens	1.93
Doubles		Jody Reed	45 (T)
Cy Young	1991	Roger Clemens	
ERA		Roger Clemens	2.62
Strikeouts		Roger Clemens	241
ERA	1992	Roger Clemens	2.41

1992 Leaders

Category	Player	
Batting Average	Tom Brunansky	.266
Home Runs	Tom Brunansky	15
RBI	Tom Brunansky	74
Stolen Bases	Jody Reed	7
Doubles	Tom Brunansky	31
Triples	Wade Boggs	4
Runs	Jody Reed	64
Hits	Wade Boggs	133
Wins	Roger Clemens	18
ERA	Roger Clemens	2.41
Strikeouts	Roger Clemens	208
Saves	Jeff Reardon	27

CLEVELAND INDIANS

It was September 29, 1954, and the Cleveland Indians were on top of the baseball world. They had been one of the American League's strongest teams for several years, but 1954 was the year it all came together.

They had just set an AL record with 111 regular season wins and finally dethroned the New York Yankees, who had won five straight championships. Cleveland confidently entered the World Series and set their sights on putting away the National League Champion New York Giants.

It was the top of the eighth in Game 1, and the score was tied 2-2. The Indians had two runners on base, nobody out, and Vic Wertz, who already had three hits in the game, was at bat.

Wertz smacked a long fly ball to center field. As the ball soared deep into the cavernous reaches of the Polo Grounds, it appeared that the Indians were about to break the game wide open and continue their season-long dominance over all who crossed their path.

Then, something amazing happened. A young outfielder named Willie Mays streaked back 460 feet and made one of the most incredible catches ever seen, an over the shoulder basket catch. The Indians were stunned. They didn't score that inning, the Giants won the game in the tenth, and went on to a four-game World Series sweep.

The Indians, to this day, have not recovered from that catch.

They finished second as late as 1959, and the Indians challenged a few times in the '60s. Since divisional play began in 1969, the Indians have never finished higher than fourth place.

Cleveland teams weren't always at the bottom of their league. The Indians won their first world championship in 1920, the year following the Black Sox World Series fix.

To say they suffered adversity in the 1920 season is a vast understatement. Midway through the season, shortstop Ray Chapman was killed by a pitched ball to his head. Led by player-manager Tris Speaker, and Chapman's replacement,

Joe Sewell, who stepped in to begin a Hall of Fame career, the Tribe persisted to win the pennant in a close race over the White Sox and the Yankees, who had acquired Babe Ruth before the season began.

The World Series that year was a wild affair won by the Indians, 5 games to 2, over the Brooklyn Dodgers. It featured Indians' second baseman Bill Wambsganss completing the only unassisted triple play in World Series history.

Over the next two decades, the best chance the Tribe had to win another title came in 1940. Despite superstar performances from 21 year old pitcher Bob Feller and rookie sensation Lou Boudreau, Cleveland fell victim to clubhouse turmoil and lost their chance for a championship.

The players, unified at a time when there was no players' union, so detested their treatment by Manager Ossie Vitt that they asked the team owners to get rid of him. The owners ignored the players' unprecedented demand, and the Indians and Vitt limped to a second place finish, one game behind the Detroit Tigers.

Cleveland won a world championship in 1948 after winning a tight three team race for the pennant. This time the opponents were the Red Sox and the Yankees. The Indians and Red Sox finished the regular season in a tie, the first time this had ever happened in AL history. In a one-game pennant deciding playoff, the Indians routed the Sox 8-3 to win the AL title.

The 1948 World Series pitted the Tribe against the Boston Braves and Cleveland won it 4 games to 2. Game 1 featured staff ace Feller against Boston's Johnny Sain. The game was scoreless heading into the eighth inning, when the Braves scored the game's only run thanks to a disputed umpiring call on a pickoff play at second base. The play cost Feller a chance at winning a World Series game, something he would never accomplish.

Recent Indians teams, in their quest to get back to the top, have developed many young stars, only to see free agency and trades send them off to become stars on other teams. The 1992 team was filled with many young and promising players such as Carlos Baerga, Kenny Lofton, Albert Belle, Sandy Alomar, Jr., and Charles Nagy.

After watching the Twins and Braves come from last to first in 1991, Tribe fans know it's not impossible. With all the present team's young talent and a new stadium on the horizon, a return to the glory days in Cleveland might not be far off.

Division Finishes 1983-1992

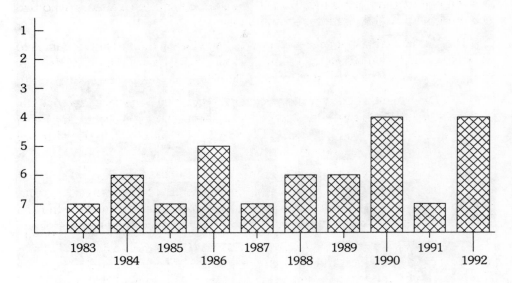

League Leaders 1983-1992

Category	Year	Leader	
Strikeouts	1985	Bert Blyleven *	206
RBI	1986	Joe Carter	121
Triples		Brett Butler	14
Rookie of the Year	1990	Sandy Alomar	
Stolen Bases	1992	Kenny Lofton	66

* Also pitched for Minnesota in 1985.

1992 Leaders

Category	Player	
Batting Average	Carlos Baerga	.312
Home Runs	Albert Belle	34
RBI	Albert Belle	112
Stolen Bases	Kenny Lofton	66
Doubles	Carlos Baerga	32
Triples	Kenny Lofton	8
Runs	Kenny Lofton	96
Hits	Carlos Baerga	205
Wins	Charles Nagy	17
ERA	Charles Nagy	2.96
Strikeouts	Charles Nagy	169
Saves	Steve Olin	29

Solution on page 137.

ACROSS

3. Player-manager of the 1920 championship Indians, Tris _____ .

6. Indians' logo, Chief _____ .

8. 1948 American League MVP, Lou _____ .

11. This Blue Jay pitcher no-hit the Indians in 1990.

12. His promising pitching career was stopped in 1957 when a line drive hit him in the eye, Herb _____ .

14. The "Immortal" Indian catcher of the 1960's.

16. He hurled a perfect game against Toronto in 1981 (two words).

17. Catcher acquired from the Yankees in 1989 for Mel Hall, Joel _____ .

18. Strikeout artist from the 1960's, Sudden Sam _____ .

19. His long pitching career began with the Indians in 1963 and lasted until 1989, Tommy _____ .

20. Hard hitting Tribe infielder from 1983-88, Julio _____ .

24. Tribe Bullpen ace in 1991 and 1992, Steve _____ .

25. He won three games in the 1920 World Series, Hall of Famer Stan _____ .

26. In his playing days Mike Hargrove was known as the Human Rain _____ .

28. He led the Tribe in homers and RBI in 1991 and 1992, Albert _____ .

31. He blasted 32 homers and 126 RBI for the 1954 AL Champion Indians, Larry _____ .

32. Led the AL in batting with .341 for the 1954 league champs, Bobby _____ .

33. This second baseman hit .306 for the Tribe in 1986, Tony _____ .

34. He roamed centerfield for the Tribe from 1984 to 1987, Brett _____ .

35. Cleveland third baseman whose great fielding plays are credited with stopping Joe DiMaggio's 56 game hitting streak, Ken _____ .

36. This Indian hit four homers in a game in 1959, _____ Colavito.

37. He led the AL with a 2.64 ERA in 1954, Mike _____ .

38. Movie which satirized the Indians losing ways, *Major* _____ .

DOWN

1. Manager of the 1954 AL champions, Al _____ .

2. Indians' 1948 World Series opponent.

4. Power hitting first baseman of the early fifties, Luke _____ .

5. In 1975 he became the first black major league manager.

7. Great Indian hurler of the '30s and '40s, Mel _____ .

9. Hall of Fame Cleveland outfielder of the 1930's, Earl _____ .

10. He picked 9 wins in relief for the Tribe in 1992, Eric _____ .

13. Starred for the Indians for six seasons before being traded to San Diego in 1990, Joe _____ .

14. The American League's All Star catcher since 1990, Sandy _____ .

15. Knuckleballer shipped off to Toronto in 1991, Tom _____ .

16. This turn-of-the-century player was so popular they called the team the "Naps" in his honor, Napoleon _____ .

21. His Tribe career fizzled after he was named 1980 AL Rookie of the Year, Joe _____ .

22. Centerfielder traded to the Pirates in 1992, Alex _____ .

23. Rapid Robert.

27. His 3.30 ERA in 1930 placed second in the American League behind only Lefty Grove, Wes _____ .

28. In 1920, he hit the first home run ever by a pitcher in a World Series game, Jim _____ .

29. Runner up for 1992 AL Rookie of the Year, Kenny _____ .

30. 1992 All Star second baseman, Carlos _____ .

32. A Cleveland favorite from the late '70's and early '80's, _____ Thornton.

# DETROIT TIGERS

Detroit had a major league baseball team as early as the 1880's, but the city was not represented in the twelve-team National League of the 1890's. This made Detroit a logical candidate for a team in Ban Johnson's new American League.

Former Baltimore Oriole shortstop Hughie Jennings became manager of the Tigers in 1907 and immediately led the team to three straight American League pennants. Hall of Famer Sam Crawford provided steady offensive power to the Tigers, but the team was utterly dominated by the personality and brilliant play of Ty Cobb.

Cobb was a fierce competitor who would do anything to win, even if it meant sharpening his spikes to intimidate and injure opposing fielders with his feet-first slides. He was the greatest hitter and base stealer of his time, arguably of all time. He won twelve batting titles and stole 892 bases, the major league record until Lou Brock passed it a half-century later. Cobb's .367 lifetime batting average still ranks first on the all-time list.

One of the few things Cobb couldn't do was lead his team to a World Series championship. His postseason failures were magnified as the Tigers lost three straight to their National League rivals from 1907 to 1909.

The first world championship for the Tigers came in 1935. They beat the Cubs in six games. Player-manager Mickey Cochrane led a solid lineup that included Hall of Famers Hank Greenberg, Charlie Gehringer, and Goose Goslin.

Greenberg is one of the all-time Tiger favorites. In 1938, he blasted 58 home runs, and in 1945, he put the Tigers back in the World Series with a dramatic, pennant clinching ninth-inning grand slam on the last day of the season.

"Hammerin' Hank" also contributed two homers in the World Series that year, and Hal Newhouser, Detroit's two-time MVP, picked up two victories as the Tigers defeated the Cubs in seven games.

In 1968, the Tigers enjoyed a banner year. After narrowly missing the pennant the year before in a tight four-team race, they came back strong to win 102 games and take the pennant in a walk. Denny McLain was certainly the standout Tiger that year. He won 31 games, more wins than any pitcher since Lefty Grove won that many in 1931.

The season of 1968 was known as the "Year of the Pitcher" as moundsmen dominated batters to an extent never before seen. Both batting averages and earned run averages dropped. Pitchers were generally perceived as having an unfair advantage, an advantage that was rectified the following year when pitching mounds were lowered.

In this poor hitting climate, the Tiger offense set no records but packed enough punch to keep them in front. Long-time Tiger outfielder great Al Kaline finally made it to the World Series, and Willie Horton, Norm Cash, Bill Freehan, and Jim Northrup all had good years at the plate.

In the World Series, the Tigers met the defending World Champion St. Louis Cardinals, who were led by Bob Gibson and his crushing 1.12 ERA. The eagerly anticipated pitching match-up between Gibson and McLain was clearly won by Gibson, who beat the Tiger ace twice, punctuating Game 1 with a record-setting 17 strikeouts. Fortunately for the Tigers, their other pitching star rose to the occasion. Mickey Lolich fought back with three victories, including a Game 7 complete game win over Gibson that gave the Tigers the championship.

The Tigers dominated the baseball world in 1984. Sparky Anderson's stars put together career years, and Anderson got big contributions from several surprise stars.

Starting pitchers Jack Morris, Milt Wilcox, and Dan Petry posted a combined 54-27 record, but the true star of the pitching staff was reliever Willie Hernandez, who earned both the Cy Young and MVP awards for his 1984 performance. The offense, too, was awesome, with a balanced attack led by Kirk Gibson, Chet Lemon, Lance Parrish, and Darrell Evans. The infield duo of Alan Trammell and Lou Whitaker was never better, and a strong Tiger bench included Ruppert Jones and Barbaro Garbey.

The Tigers led the AL East from day one and never looked back. They won the division by fifteen games, made quick work of Kansas City in the playoffs, and then rolled past the San Diego Padres in the World Series, four games to one.

The World Series of 1984 provided baseball with one of the great "what if" debates since the Chicago Cubs were generally regarded as the strongest team in the National League but inexplicably blew the Championship Series and lost to the opportunistic Padres. While it is doubtful that anyone could have derailed the Detroit juggernaut in 1984, a Tigers-Cubs Series would have had the historical significance of matching two teams that had met in the fall classic four times previously, a rarity these days.

The Tigers won the AL East again in 1987 in an exciting down to the wire race with the Toronto Blue Jays. They were bested in the playoffs by the eventual World Champion Minnesota Twins.

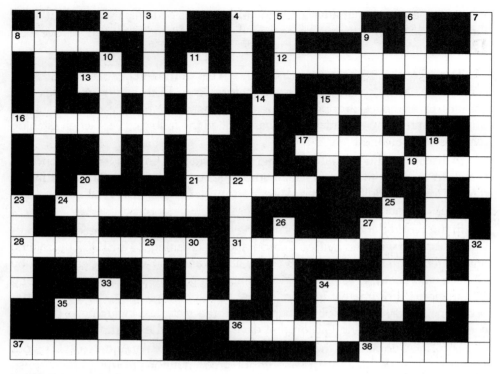

Solution on page 137.

ACROSS

1. His best year for the Tigers was a 22-8 mark for the 1934 American League champs, Schoolboy _____ .
4. This Tiger great retired in 1974 after collecting 3007 lifetime hits.
8. This Hall of Famer played third base for the Tigers from 1946 to 1952, George _____ .
12. This Tiger speedster stole 78 bases in 1979 (two words).
13. This Tiger outfielder led the 1968 World Champions in runs batted in with 90, Jim _____ .
15. Detroit's bullpen ace since 1987, Mike _____ .
16. 20 game winner for the Tigers in 1991, Bill _____ .
17. The first of three baseball generations, he played third for the Tigers in the fifties, Ray _____ .

19. Tiger right fielder and long ball threat, Rob _____ .
21. Well travelled hurler who was the pitching star for the Tigers in the 1940 World Series, Bobo _____ .
24. He pitched in four World Series for the Tigers and had a 4-1 record, Tommy _____ .
27. He went 9 and 0 for the Tigers in the 1987 stretch run, _____ Alexander.
28. Second baseman for the 1968 World Champion Tigers, Dick _____ .
31. Led the Tigers in stolen bases in 1991 with 41, Milt _____ .
34. Detroit Hall of Famer, Wahoo Sam _____ .
35. Shortstop for the 1984 World Champion Tigers.
36. Right fielder for the 1984 World Champion Tigers.
37. Catcher for the 1968 World Champion Tigers.

38. Former name of Tiger Stadium.

DOWN

1. This Tiger pitching great was inducted into the Hall of Fame in 1992.
3. This Tiger second baseman had a great offensive season in 1992, Lou _____ .
4. This Tiger outfielder hit .318 with 26 homers and 105 RBI in 1979, Steve _____ .
5. Detroit's Yankee Killer, Frank _____ .
6. He set a major league record for saves in 1973 which lasted for ten years, John _____ .
7. Tiger Hall of Famer, Hammerin' Hank _____ .
9. This Hall of Famer managed the Tigers to three straight pennants in 1907-1909, Hugh _____ .
10. He won three games in the 1968 World Series, Mickey _____ .
11. He shared third base duties with Howard Johnson for the 1984 World Champion Tigers, Tom _____ .
14. Tiger pinch hitting specialist from the sixties, _____ Brown.

15. This Tiger outfielder batted .323 with 21 homers and 103 RBI in 1950, _____ Evers.
18. This catcher blasted 30-plus homers for the Tigers in 1991 and 1992, Mickey _____ .
20. He won 27 games for the Tigers in 1944, Dizzy _____ .
22. He contributed 17 wins to the Tigers' winning effort in 1984, Milt _____ .
23. Centerfielder for the 1984 World Champion Tigers, Chet _____ .
25. Detroit record label.
26. The Georgia Peach (two words).
29. This Tiger shortstop knocked in 96 runs in 1992, Travis _____ .
30. He led the Tiger pitching staff with 22 wins in 1967, _____ Wilson.
32. Tigers' opponents in the 1984 World Series.
33. This Tiger first baseman batted .361 in 1961, Norm _____ .
34. He played short for the Tigers in the late fifties, _____ Veal.

Division Finishes 1983-1992

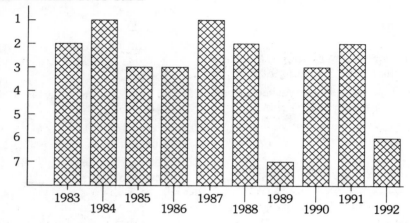

League Leaders 1983-1992

Category	Year	Leader	
Strikeouts	1983	Jack Morris	232
MVP	1984	Willie Hernandez	
Cy Young		Willie Hernandez	
Home Runs	1985	Darrell Evans	40
Home Runs	1990	Cecil Fielder	51
RBI		Cecil Fielder	132
Home Runs	1991	Cecil Fielder	44 (T)
RBI		Cecil Fielder	133
Wins		Bill Gullickson	20 (T)
RBI	1992	Cecil Fielder	124
Runs		Tony Phillips	114

1992 Leaders

Category	Player	
Batting Average	Lou Whitaker	.278
Home Runs	Cecil Fielder	35
RBI	Cecil Fielder	124
Stolen Bases	Tony Phillips	12
Doubles	Tony Phillips	32
Triples	Travis Fryman	4
Runs	Tony Phillips	114
Hits	Travis Fryman	175
Wins	Bill Gullickson	14
ERA	Bill Gullickson	4.34
Strikeouts	Frank Tanana	91
Saves	Mike Henneman	24

MILWAUKEE BREWERS

The 1969 season was the only time in baseball history that both major leagues expanded at the same time. Four new teams were added that year, bringing the total to twenty four and necessitating the replacement of two ten-team leagues with four six-team divisions. The new entries that year were the Montreal Expos, San Diego Padres, Kansas City Royals, and Seattle Pilots.

Baseball in Seattle started off with a bang. The Pilots won their first game ever, defeating the Angels at Anaheim 4-3. They also won their first two home games against Chicago, giving them a 3-1 record out of the box. That was the peak of the season, though. The remainder of the season, as well as the team's relationship with the City of Seattle, went downhill from there.

The offensive stars of the Pilots were Tommy Harper, who led the league that year with 73 stolen bases, Don Mincher, who blasted 25 homers, and a surprising late-season call up named Greg Goossen, who finished strong with 10 homers and a .309 average.

The pitching corps was led by Gene Brabender. He set a record for expansion team victories with 13. They also had a knuckleball pitcher who carried around a notebook and told people he was writing a book. His name was Jim Bouton, and his book, *Ball Four*, came out the following year to the chagrin of the baseball establishment.

The Pilots played their home games in Sicks' Stadium, a rickety ballpark which became the focus of controversy between the city fathers and the team's management, who expected faster progress on a new domed stadium. Although the Pilots drew well, the animosity resulted in a sudden and surprise shift of the franchise to Milwaukee just four days before the start of the 1970 season.

Milwaukee fans, who had witnessed the Braves move to Atlanta just five years earlier , were ecstatic to have major league baseball back in town, and the team drew just short of a million fans its first season. On the field, the team, now called the Brewers, finished in a fourth place tie in the AL West.

An early hero for the Brewers was outfielder Danny Walton, who became the team's hitting star in the early part of the 1970 season but suffered a mid-season knee injury, from which he never fully recovered.

In 1972, the Washington Senators moved to Texas to become the Rangers, and in the AL's realignment, the Brewers were moved to the Eastern Division where they remain today. Through most of the 1970's, the Brewers generally fielded poor teams at a time when the AL East was considered the strongest division in baseball. One highlight during this period was the return to Milwaukee of Hank Aaron, who finished his illustrious career with the Brewers in 1976.

In 1978, under new manager George Bamberger, the Brewers had their first winning season. They finished with a very respectable 93-69 record, but that was only good enough for third place in the East, 6 1/2 games behind the eventual World Champion New York Yankees. This season saw the beginnings of the team that would make it to the World Series four years later. The offense was led by the bats of Larry Hisle, Gorman Thomas, Ben Ogilvie, and Cecil Cooper. The team was anchored by a trio of young infielders named Robin Yount, Paul Molitor, and Jim Gantner who would remain Brewer teammates through the 1990's.

The 1979 Brewers improved to a 95-66 record, their best season record ever. Unfortunately for them, Earl Weaver's Orioles won 102 games that year and took the pennant.

In 1981, the Brewers finally finished the season in first place, but in the strike-interrupted season that was only good enough for one-half of the AL East crown and the right to play the Yankees in the best-of-five "Division Playoffs."

With the series tied two games apiece, the Brewers led the fifth game by a 2-0 score over Yankee ace Ron Guidry. However, the Yankee bats exploded for three homers, and the Yankees took the game and the AL East title.

The Brewers bounced back the next year to win their first American League pennant. Harvey Kuenn took the Brewers' helm midway through the season. His "Harvey's Wallbangers," led by MVP Robin Yount, ripped American League pitching throughout the season en route to leading the league in nearly every offensive category. The Brewers fought an uphill battle to make it to the World Series. They spotted the California Angels a 2-0 lead in the best-of-five ALCS before sweeping the remaining three games. Cecil Cooper provided the clutch single in Game 5 that sealed the pennant for the Brewers.

The Brewers suffered a disappointing World Series loss to the St. Louis Cardinals. They couldn't hold a lead in Game 7, and the Cardinals came from behind to take the championship.

The Brewers almost made it to the playoffs again in 1992. They remained in contention until the final week before being beaten by the future World Champion Blue Jays for the AL East title. The season was highlighted by all-time Brewer great Robin Yount reaching the 3,000 hit plateau.

Division Finishes 1983-1992

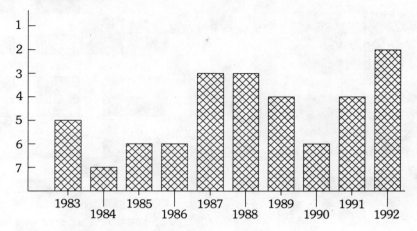

League Leaders 1983-1992

Category	Year	Leader	
RBI	1983	Cecil Cooper	126
Triples		Robin Yount	10
Doubles	1987	Paul Molitor	41
Runs		Paul Molitor	114
Triples	1988	Robin Yount	11 (T)
MVP	1989	Robin Yount	
Triples	1991	Paul Molitor	13(T)
Runs		Paul Molitor	133
Hits		Paul Molitor	216
Rookie of the Year	1992	Pat Listach	

1992 Leaders

Category	Player	
Batting Average	Paul Molitor	.340
Home Runs	Greg Vaughan	23
RBI	Paul Molitor	89
Stolen Bases	Pat Listach	54
Doubles	Robin Yount	40
Triples	Darryl Hamilton	7 (T)
	Paul Molitor	7 (T)
Runs	Pat Listach	93
Hits	Paul Molitor	195
Wins	Jaime Navarro	17
ERA	Bill Wegman	3.20
Strikeouts	Bill Wegman	127
Saves	Doug Henry	29

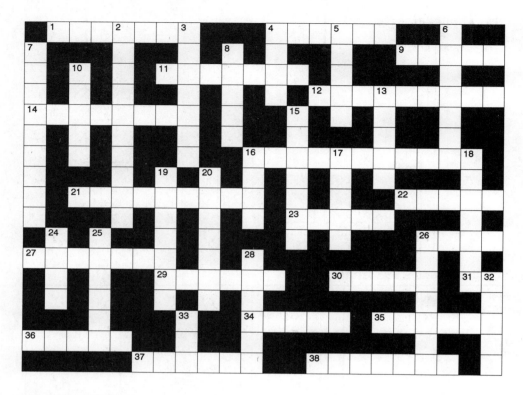

Solution on page 137.

ACROSS

1. Milwaukee's 1992 rookie phenom, Pat
   _____ .

4. He saved 33 games for the Brewers in
   1989, Dan _____ .

9. This Milwaukee first baseman led the
   AL with 36 homers and 109 RBI in
   1975, George _____ .

11. This Brewer outfielder blasted 41 hom-
    ers in 1980, Ben _____ .

12. 1982 American League Cy Young
    Award winner, Pete _____ .

14. Outfielder traded to the Colorado
    Rockies for Kevin Reimer, Dante _____ .

16. In 1982, Harvey's _____ rocked the
    American League.

21. Brewers' opponents in the 1982 World
    Series.

22. He reached the 3,000 hit plateau in
    1992.

23. Pitcher who came over from the
    Padres in the Gary Sheffield trade,
    _____ Bones.

26. What made Milwaukee famous.

27. This right-hander won 17 games for
    the Brewers in 1992, Jaime _____ .

29. This left-hander no-hit the Orioles in
    1987, Juan _____ .

30. Brewers' President who became base-
    ball's interim commissioner in 1992,
    Bud _____ .

31. Stolen base (abbrev.).

34. He DHed for the AL Champion Brew-
    ers in 1982, batting .284, Don _____ .

35. He led the 1982 AL Champion Brew-
    ers in homers with 39, Gorman _____ .

36. He saved 15 games for the Brewers in
    1991 while posting a microscopic 1.00
    ERA, Doug _____ .

37. Early Brewer favorite, Outfielder
    Danny _____ .

38. The manager of the 1969 Seattle Pilots, Joe _____ .

DOWN

2. Brewers' manager from 1987 to 1991.
3. 20 game winner for the Brewers in 1986, Ted _____ .
4. Milwaukee skipper, _____ Garner.
5. Brewer shortstop who banged out 25 homers in 1987, Dale _____ .
6. His 39-game hitting streak in 1987 was one of baseball's best.
7. This tall right-hander won 13 games for the expansion Pilots in 1969, Gene _____ .
8. This Brewer outfielder blasted 34 homers and 115 RBI in 1978, Larry_____ .
10. First baseman for the 1982 AL Champion Brewers, _____ Cooper.
13. Manager of the 1982 AL Champion Brewers.
15. In 1973 he became the first Brewer to win 20 games, Jim _____ .

16. In 1970 and 1971 the Brewers played in the AL _____ .
17. This first baseman batted .299 with 85 RBI for the 1987 Brewers, Greg_____ .
18. He saved 31 games for the Brewers back in 1971, Ken _____ .
19. Catcher for the 1982 Brewers, he faced his former teammates in that year's World Series.
20. Long time Brewer second baseman, Jim _____ .
24. He went 13-3 for the Brewers in 1983, Moose _____ .
25. 30-30 man for Milwaukee in 1970, Tommy _____ .
26. Pete Ladd, otherwise known as _____ , saved 25 games for the Brewers in 1983.
28. He posted a 15-7 record for Milwaukee in 1991, Bill _____ .
32. He posted a 16-6 record for the 1992 Brewers, Chris _____ .
33. He won 11 and lost only 2 for the 1992 Brewers, _____ Eldred.

NEW YORK YANKEES

The Yankees are by far the most successful franchise in major league baseball history. So impressive are their achievements (33 American League pennants, 22 World Championships) that even their current dry spell of eleven years without a World Series appearance doesn't begin to put a dent in their prestige.

From 1921 through 1964, the Yankees truly dominated baseball, never going more than three years without winning a pennant that entire period.

The team began in 1903 as the New York Highlanders and nearly won the pennant in their second season. In the first two decades of the twentieth century, the Yankees were relegated to playing second fiddle in New York to John McGraw's Giants, a much more successful team both on the field and at the gate.

All of this changed for the Yankees after a one-player deal in 1920, the purchase of Babe Ruth from the Boston Red Sox. Ruth was a left-handed pitcher recently moved to the outfield. His hitting talents were so great that he would remain an everyday player for the rest of his career.

With Ruth on board, the Yankees won pennants in 1921 and 1922, but lost the World Series to the Giants each time. In 1923, the Yankees celebrated their first season in Yankee Stadium by overcoming their nemesis, the Giants, in the World Series to win their first championship.

In 1925, Lou Gehrig joined the Yankees, and the team won three more pennants from 1926 to 1928. The 1927 team won 110 games and is considered to be the best team of all time. Led by Ruth (60 homers, 164 RBI), Gehrig (47 homers, 175 RBI), Tony Lazzeri, Bob Meusel, and Earle Combs, this "Murderer's Row" led the Yankees as they swept the Pittsburgh Pirates 4-0 in the World Series.

In 1932, the Yankees again swept the World Series. Their opponents in '32 were the Cubs, and the series is most famous for Babe Ruth's legendary "called shot" against Cub pitcher Charlie Root.

By 1936, Ruth had retired, but the Yankees had a rookie sensation, Joe DiMaggio, who led the team to four consecutive world championships from 1936 through 1939, losing only three World Series games along the way.

By 1939, Gehrig had established himself as the greatest first baseman of all time and set a longevity record of 2,130 consecutive games. That year a rare muscle disease tragically ended his career and, soon afterward, his life. On July 4, 1939, the Yankees honored their beloved captain with a special ceremony, and Gehrig, in baseball's most emotional moment, called himself the luckiest man on the face of the earth.

In 1941, DiMaggio thrilled baseball with his 56-game hitting streak and the Yankees defeated the Brooklyn Dodgers in the World Series, something they would do five more times over the next fifteen years.

After a third place finish by the Yankees in 1948, manager Bucky Harris was fired. The Yankees chose Casey Stengel to replace Harris, a seemingly odd choice considering the fact that Stengel's stints as manager of the Dodgers and the Braves had been largely unsuccessful.

The Yankees won a close pennant race in 1949 and beat the Dodgers in the World Series. Little did anyone realize then that the Yankees were on the verge of the greatest baseball dynasty of all time.

Stengel's teams won five straight world championships in his first five years as Yankee manager. His managerial moves were often brilliant. He platooned players at several positions to maximize his talent. It also helped that he had players like Yogi Berra, Mickey Mantle, Whitey Ford, and a seemingly endless parade of pitchers who always got the clutch win, and hitters who always got the clutch hit.

By 1960, Stengel had managed the Yankees for twelve years and won ten pennants, but after losing a hard fought World Series to the Pirates, Casey was let go. The reason given for Stengel's dismissal was that he was too old. Ralph Houk took the helm in 1961 and continued the pace by reeling off three more pennants, and first year manager Yogi Berra added one more in 1964.

The roof fell in after 1964. Johnny Keane took over the manager's seat in 1965 after Berra was fired, and witnessed the collapse of the Yankee dynasty as age, slumps, and injuries finally took their toll on the pinstripers. Also in '65, baseball began a player draft system which served to distribute talent around the major leagues more evenly, thus effectively killing the possibility of ever again seeing a Yankee-like dynasty.

Nevertheless, the Bronx Bombers returned to glory once again in the late seventies. New owner George Steinbrenner built these Yankees by actively pursuing free agents, signing such stars as Reggie Jackson, Catfish Hunter, Goose Gossage, and Dave Winfield. This approach helped the Yankees capture world championships in 1977 and 1978 and American League pennants in 1976 and 1981.

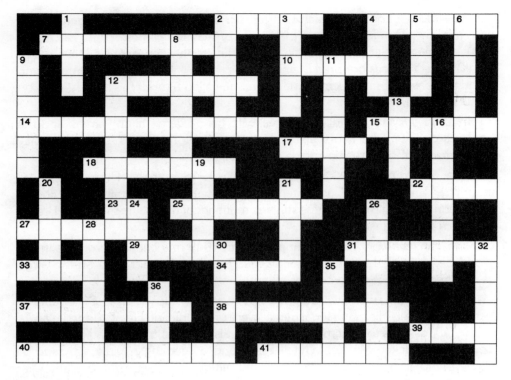

Solution on page 138.

ACROSS

2. During his long Yankee career he played in 14 World Series.

3. He won 13 for the Yankees in 1992 after coming over from the White Sox, _____ Perez.

7. After a superb 12-2 season at Columbus, this right-hander was called up to the Yankees in mid-1992 and won his first two starts, Sam _____ .

10. Yankee outfielder from the early sixties, Hector _____ .

12. The Scooter.

14. Controversial Yankee owner, George _____ .

15. Cy Young Award winner in 1978 with a 25-3 record and a 1.74 ERA.

17. The Sultan of Swat.

18. He struck out an AL leading 217 batters in 1964 while helping the Yanks win another pennant, Al _____ .

22. The Yankees' ace fireman from the late forties, Joe _____ .

23. Pinch runner (abbrev.).

25. Yankee first baseman from 1954 to 1962, Moose _____ .

27. Twenty game winner for the Yanks in 1949, 1950, and 1951, Vic _____ .

29. Old time Yankee first baseman often accused of throwing games, Hal _____ .

31. He no-hit the White Sox in 1990 but lost 4-0, Andy _____ .

33. His fabled homer over the left field wall in Boston capped an incredible 1978 stretch run.

34. Yankee infielder from the sixties and harmonica soloist, Phil _____ .

37. Tall left-hander who pitched for the Yankees in the sixties, Steve _____ .

38. He blasted 25 Homers for the Yanks in 1992, Danny _____ .

39. Lou Gehrig, the _____ Horse.

40. Yankee second baseman from the 1960's, Bobby _____ .
41. He replaced the Babe in right field in 1935, George _____ .

DOWN

1. Lou Gehrig replaced him at first base in 1925 and went on to play in 2,130 consecutive games, Wally _____ .
2. This hard thrower won 21 games for the 1963 Yankees, Jim _____ .
3. Yankee third baseman during their late-thirties dynasty years, Red _____ .
4. This Hall of Fame slugger was an important clutch hitter for the Yankees of 1949-1953, Johnny _____ .
5. Yankee reliever who won the 1977 Cy Young Award.
6. This Yankee hurler got bombed by the Bucs in the 1960 World series, losing 2 games, Art _____ .
8. Yankee second baseman during the Murderers' Row years, Tony _____ .
9. His perfect game in 1956 was one of the all time greatest World Series feats, Don _____ .
11. George Brett put too much of this on his bat, then homered, causing a 1983 furor.

12. Yankee second baseman from 1976 to 1988.
13. Became Yankee manager in 1992, _____ Showalter.
16. Joltin' Joe.
19. Led the Yankees in homers in 1991 with 24, Matt _____ .
20. He came over to manage the Yankees in 1965 and watched the dynasty crumble, Johnny _____ .
21. Hall of Fame Yankee hurler from the 1930's, Lefty _____ .
24. Catcher for the 1981 AL champs, _____ Cerone.
26. His lifetime record for the Yankees was 109 wins and 43 losses, an all time record for winning pct., Spud _____ .
28. He won 23 games for the Yankees in 1975 after escaping Charlie Finley's A's through free agency, _____ Hunter.
30. He was the American League MVP in 1963, _____ Howard.
32. Catcher for pennant-winning Yankee teams in 1921, 1922 and 1923, Wally _____ .
35. Yankee shortstop from 1957 to 1965, Tony _____ .
36. This Yankee pitching ace was inducted into the Hall of Fame in 1974 together with Mickey Mantle.

Division Finishes 1983-1992

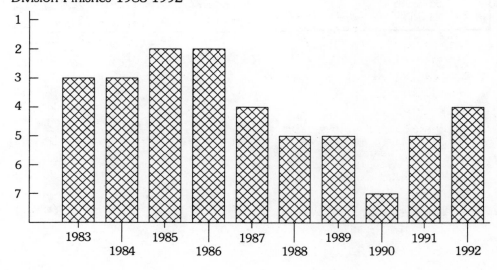

League Leaders 1983-1992

Category	Year	Leader	
Batting Average	1984	Don Mattingly	.343
Doubles		Don Mattingly	44
Hits		Don Mattingly	207
MVP	1985	Don Mattingly	
RBI		Don Mattingly	145
Wins		Ron Guidry	22
Winning Pct.		Ron Guidry	.786 (22-6)
Stolen Bases		Rickey Henderson	80
Doubles		Don Mattingly	48
Runs		Rickey Henderson	146
Stolen Bases	1986	Rickey Henderson	87
Saves		Dave Righetti	46
Doubles		Don Mattingly	53
Runs		Rickey Henderson	130
Hits		Don Mattingly	238
Stolen Bases	1988	Rickey Henderson	93
Stolen Bases	1989	Rickey Henderson *	77
Runs		Rickey Henderson *	113 (T)

*Also played for Oakland in 1989.

1992 Leaders

Category	Player	
Batting Average	Don Mattingly	.287
Home Runs	Danny Tartabull	25
RBI	Don Mattingly	86
Stolen Bases	Roberto Kelly	28
Doubles	Don Mattingly	40
Triples	Mel Hall	3
Runs	Don Mattingly	89
Hits	Don Mattingly	184
Wins	Melido Perez	13
ERA	Melido Perez	2.87
Strikeouts	Melido Perez	218
Saves	Steve Farr	30

TORONTO
BLUE JAYS

The Blue Jays joined the American League in 1977 along with the Seattle Mariners in the league's second expansion in eight years. The year before, Toronto almost became the home of the San Francisco Giants, but the deal fell through. Toronto fans are no doubt thankful, considering the enormous success the Blue Jays have had in just 16 seasons.

The team played its home games at a converted football field called Exhibition Stadium, where they remained until the opening of the beautiful new Skydome in 1989.

Under early managers Roy Hartsfield and Bobby Mattick, the Jays finished in last place their first five years, but the club quietly assembled a scouting and development system that made them contenders after only seven seasons.

In 1983, manager Bobby Cox's team won 89 games behind the pitching of Dave Steib, the hitting of Willie Upshaw and Lloyd Moseby, and the speed of Damaso Garcia and Dave Collins. This season was a turning point, and the Blue Jays have never had a losing season since.

The following year, the Jays posted an identical 89-73 record, second place in the American League East, but still a distant fifteen games behind the champion Detroit Tigers.

The Blue Jays continued to improve. By 1985, George Bell, Jesse Barfield, Tony Fernandez and Jimmy Key were added to the line up. Now a legitimate power in the AL East, Toronto won their first division title by edging out the Yankees in a close race.

They entered their first postseason series with great optimism, but the collapse in the 1985 ALCS against the Royals proved to be only the first in a number of late-season failures that would frustrate the Jays for years.

The Jays got off to a strong start, taking three of the first four games. Any other year, this would have clinched the pennant, but in 1985, the league playoffs were extended from a best-of-five to a best-of-seven affair. The Royals capitalized by sweeping the remaining three games for the pennant.

If 1985 was disappointing for the Blue Jays, then 1987 was devastating. They blew a division title by losing their last seven games of the season. The clincher was a humbling three-game sweep at the hands of the Tigers the final weekend.

After a slow start in 1989, Cito Gaston replaced Jimy Williams as manager in May and sparked the team to the top of the division once again. A few weeks later, the new Skydome opened. The combination of an exciting team and the new ballpark helped generate an incredible three million in attendance for the season. Steib led the starters with 17 wins, and the bullpen was solid with right-hander Tom Henke and left-hander Duane Ward. Big contributions were made that year by sluggers McGriff, Bell, and third baseman Kelly Gruber. Disappointingly, the Jays came up short in the playoffs again, this time losing to the Rickey Henderson-led A's in five games.

In 1991, the Blue Jays underwent major changes, and they bounced back to win the division. Gone were Bell, McGriff and Fernandez, and new stars Roberto Alomar, Joe Carter and Devon White were brought in. Rookie Juan Guzman became a reliable starter joining Key, Todd Stottlemyre and David Wells. This time, the Twins toppled the Jays in the ALCS.

Finally, the Blue Jays put it all together in 1992. They knew they possessed the talent and confidence to win, it was just a matter of shaking the spectre of past post-season failures. Free agents Dave Winfield and Jack Morris were signed, and these veteran superstars led Toronto back to the playoffs.

Toronto GM Pat Gillick sought help at pitcher for the stretch drive for the pennant. He dealt two young prospects to the Mets for star pitcher David Cone. The addition of Cone made the Jays' pitching staff too strong for the others to catch them.

Despite an embarrassing 22-2 loss to the Brewers and nearly being no-hit by Boston's Frank Viola, the Jays held off both the Orioles and the Brewers. The ALCS brought together the Jays with the A's in a rematch of the 1989 championship series, but this time Toronto took it in six games.

The Blue Jays lost Game 1 of the World Series to Atlanta, as Morris suffered his first postseason loss. Toronto then reeled off three straight one-run victories, highlighted by Ed Sprague's game-winning homer in Game 2, Candy Maldonado's clutch ninth inning RBI in Game 3, and Jimmy Key's strong pitching performance in Game 4.

Morris took the mound in Game 5 and was again blasted by the Braves, but the 41 year old Winfield came through with a clutch double in the eleventh inning of Game 6 to give the Blue Jays their long awaited first World Championship. Catcher Pat Borders shined throughout the Series, and was named World Series MVP.

Division Finishes 1983-1992

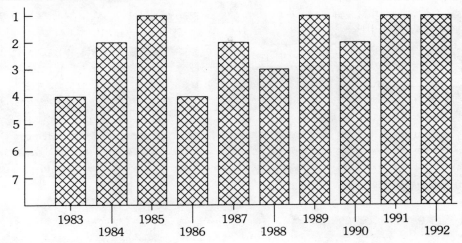

League Leaders 1983-1992

Category	Year	Leader	
Winning Pct.	1984	Doyle Alexander	.739 (17-6)
Triples		Dave Collins	15 (T)
		Lloyd Moseby	15 (T)
ERA	1985	Dave Stieb	2.48
Home Runs	1986	Jesse Barfield	40
MVP	1987	George Bell	
ERA		Jimmy Key	2.76
RBI		George Bell	134
Saves		Tom Henke	34
Home Runs	1989	Fred McGriff	36
Triples	1990	Tony Fernandez	17
Wins	1992	Jack Morris	21 (T)
Winning Pct.		Jack Morris	.778 (21-6)

1992 Leaders

Category	Player	
Batting Average	Roberto Alomar	.310
Home Runs	Joe Carter	34
Runs Batted In	Joe Carter	19
Stolen Bases	Roberto Alomar	49
Doubles	Dave Winfield	33
Triples	Roberto Alomar	8
Runs	Roberto Alomar	105
Hits	Roberto Alomar	177
Wins	Jack Morris	21
ERA	Juan Guzman	2.64
Strikeouts	Juan Guzman	165
Saves	Tom Henke	34

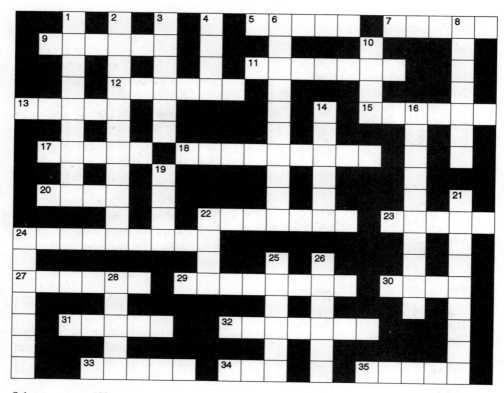

Solution on page 138.

ACROSS

5. His great catch in Game 3 of the 1992 World Series nearly started a triple play, Devon _____ .

7. Rocket-armed rightfielder for the Blue Jays in the mid-eighties, _____ Barfield.

9. He knocked in 119 runs for the Blue Jays in 1992.

11. Toronto infielder who was named American League Rookie of the Year in 1979, Alfredo _____ .

12. He has excelled in bases-loaded situations throughout his career, Blue Jay pinch hitter Pat _____ .

13. Blue Jays' catcher from 1977 to 1989, Ernie _____ .

15. Blue Jay's first baseman who hit .284 in 1992, John _____ .

17. He has 174 lifetime wins as a Blue Jay, Dave _____ .

18. Toronto third baseman in the mid-1980's, Rance _____ .

20. Blue Jay manager from 1986 to mid-1989, _____ Williams.

22. 1992 World Series MVP, Pat _____ .

23. This pitcher went 7 and 0 for the 1985 AL East Champion Blue Jays, Tom _____ .

24. This second baseman's best year for the Jays was 1988 when he batted .291 (two words).

27. This right-hander went 16 and 5 for the 1992 Jays, Juan _____ .

29. This pitcher was picked up from Baltimore for the Blue Jays' 1987 stretch drive, Mike _____ .

30. Blue Jay power hitter from the early days, _____ Mayberry.

31. Toronto's bullpen ace from 1985-1992, Tom _____ .

32. Second baseman for the 1989 AL East Champion Blue Jays, Nelson _____ .

33. This big left-hander won 15 games for the Jays in 1991, David _____ .
34. His best year for the Blue Jays was 1987 when he won 17 and lost 8, Jimmy _____ .
35. Toronto picked up this pitcher from Cleveland for the 1990 stretch run, Bud _____ .

DOWN

1. Toronto picked up this pitcher from Cleveland for the 1991 stretch run, Tom _____ .
2. His father, Mel, pitched for the Yankees, Todd _____ .
3. This Toronto third baseman knocked in 118 runs in 1990.
4. Toronto picked up this pitcher from the Mets for the 1992 stretch run, David _____ .
6. The Blue Jays' first manager, Roy _____ .
8. When Dave Winfield was a Yankee, he once caused a furor in Toronto by hitting one of these creatures in mid-flight.

10. Toronto skipper, _____ Gaston.
14. He batted .310 for the expansion Blue Jays in 1977, Bob _____ .
16. Home of the Blue Jays until 1989, _____ Stadium.
19. A fixture in the Jays' starting rotation in the early 1980's, Luis _____ .
21. He won 13 games for the expansion Blue Jays in 1977, Dave _____ .
22. All Star outfielder for the Blue Jays in the eighties, George _____ .
24. First baseman for the 1989 AL East Champion Blue Jays, Fred _____ .
25. This veteran did most of the DHing for the expansion Jays of 1977, Ron _____ .
26. Second baseman for Toronto's 1985 division championship team, _____ Garcia.
28. He played the infield for the Blue Jays in 1979-81 then left baseball for a career in the NBA.

CALIFORNIA ANGELS

After the Dodgers and Giants pioneered the way to California in 1958, the American League grew eager to plant a team of its own there. The instant success of the former New York teams prompted the AL's first-ever expansion. In 1961, the Los Angeles Angels entered the league along with the new Washington Senators.

The Angels had planned to play their home games at the Dodgers' brand new stadium at Chavez Ravine, but the stadium wasn't ready until 1962. In their haste to field a team for 1961, the Angels settled on Wrigley Field, a former minor league park, to be their temporary home.

Wrigley Field (once owned by the Chicago Cubs, as the name suggests) was a hitters' paradise with short outfield fences. To take advantage of its friendly dimensions the Angels went into the expansion draft looking for sluggers. They came out with Ted Kluszewski, Leon Wagner, Bob Cerv, Steve Bilko and Ken Hunt.

When the season was over, they amassed a total of 189 home runs, second only to the Yankees who set an all time record that year with 240. The season of 1961 was also the year of Roger Maris' record-breaking 61 homers. Curiously, he hit only two of them at Wrigley.

The first-year Angels won 70 games and finished in eighth place. Their second year, 1962, they moved to Chavez Ravine and exceeded everyone's expectations by winning 86 games and finishing third, just 10 games behind the World Champion Yankees.

Eighty-six wins for an expansion team was incredible. For example, other newcomers like the Mets and Senators were regularly finishing in last place and showing no signs of improving.

Their on-field success didn't seem to matter, however, when it came to building a fan base. The Angels were undeniably second class citizens in LA. The Dodgers were tremendously popular. They won pennants in 1963 and 1965, just missed one in 1962, and regularly drew two million fans a year, usually about three times what the Angels drew in the same ballpark.

The Angels took their first step toward independence in 1965 when they changed their name to the California Angels. In 1966, they left the shadow of the Dodgers and moved to their own new stadium in Anaheim.

In the seventies, when players began to exercise their new-found status as free agents, the Angels were one of the first teams to actively pursue them. They signed luminaries Bobby Grich, Joe Rudi, Don Baylor, Lyman Bostock, and Rod Carew.

Unfortunately for the Angels, they always had great teams on paper, but could never sustain any type of dominance. Over the years, they have won their division three times, only to come back each following year with a losing record.

The first American League West title for the Angels came in 1979. Led by their new manager, former Angel star Jim Fregosi, the Angels blended young and old, with veterans Carew, Baylor, Grich and Brian Downing to go with youngsters like Carney Lansford, Willie Aikens and Dickie Thon. The pitching staff was anchored by Nolan Ryan, Dave Frost, and the bullpen tandem of Mark Clear and Dave LaRoche. Owner Gene Autry's high-priced stars couldn't get past the Baltimore Orioles in the ALCS, though. They were beaten in four games.

By 1982, the Angels had added Reggie Jackson and Doug DeCinces to their star-studded lineup. They won their second AL West title, with a 93-69 record, their best year ever. In the best-of-five ALCS they led the Milwaukee Brewers two games to none, but their pitching gave out as they lost three straight to again fall short of a pennant.

The 1986 Angels were led by budding superstar Wally Joyner, who blasted 22 homers with 100 RBIs and a .290 batting average in his rookie season. The pitching staff was led by Mike Witt and Kirk McCaskill and seasoned veterans Don Sutton and John Candelaria. They won the American League West by five games over the Texas Rangers and faced the Boston Red Sox in the AL playoffs.

In Game 5, the Angels had a three game to one edge in the series, and took a five to four lead into the ninth inning. Donnie Moore was on the mound facing Boston's Dave Henderson, needing only one more strike to give the Angels the American League pennant. Bad luck hit the Angels again. Henderson hit a dramatic two-run homer, the Red Sox won the game in the eleventh, and put away the Angels easily in Games 6 and 7.

Finally, 1986 looked like it was going to be the Angels' year. Gene Mauch, in his twenty-fifth year of managing, looked like he was finally going to make it to the World Series. He had come close before, with the Phillies in 1964, and with the Angels in 1982. However, the 1986 season had the same sad ending once again for Mauch and the Angels' fans.

Solution on page 138.

ACROSS

6. The Angels traded this left-hander to the Yankees after the 1992 season, Jim _____.

9. The Angels' opponents in the 1982 American League Championship Series.

11. Angel bonus baby from the 1960's, Rick _____.

12. Angels right-hander who tossed four shutouts during the strike-shortened season of 1981, Ken _____.

13. He led the Angel staff with an 18-8 record in 1982 as they took the AL West title, Geoff _____.

14. All Star shortstop for the Angels in the 1960's, Jim _____.

15. He hurled a perfect game against the Rangers in 1984, Mike _____.

17. This Angel left-hander posted identical 18-9 records in 1990 and 1991, Chuck _____.

19. This right-hander won 17 games for the 1986 AL West Champion Angels, Kirk _____.

22. Angel catcher from 1982 to 1988, Bob _____.

23. California city the Angels call home.

26. He collected 31 saves for the Angels in 1985, Donnie _____.

29. Double play (abbrev.).

31. This right-hander went 17-5 for the Angels in 1989, Bert _____.

32. The American League's MVP in 1979, Don _____.

34. Early Angel outfielder Leon "_____ Wags" Wagner.

35. He was named 1992 minor league player of the year by Baseball America, outfielder Tim _____.

37. He managed the Angels to division titles in 1982 and 1986, _____ Mauch.
38. He played second base for the Angels in the sixties, Bobby _____ .
39. This Angel lefty won 19 games in 1986, Frank _____ .
40. Surprise selection by the Florida Marlins in the expansion draft, reliever Bryan _____ .
41. This Angel no-hit the Orioles in 1962, _____ Belinsky.
42. This Angel pitcher won the Cy Young Award in 1964, Dean _____ .
43. This Angel outfielder knocked in 72 runs in 1992, Junior _____ .

DOWN

1. First baseman for the 1979 AL West Champion Angels, Rod _____ .
2. This Angel second baseman hit 22 homers to lead the AL in the strike-shortened season of 1981, Bobby _____ .
3. Angels' general manager, Whitey _____ .
4. This slugger came over to the Angels from the Yankees in a 1990 trade, Dave _____ .
5. This left-hander had a 19-8 record for the Angels in 1991, Mark _____ .

7. This ill-fated Angel outfielder batted .296 in 1978, Lyman _____ .
8. Angel All Star first baseman in the early sixties, Lee _____ .
10. This shortstop was traded to the Mets in 1992 for Julio Valera, Dick _____ .
16. The first manager of the Angels in 1961, Bill _____ .
18. Third baseman for the 1982 AL West Champion Angels, Doug _____ .
20. The Angels acquired him in a trade with the Red Sox for Jerry Remy, pitcher Don _____ .
21. Before 1965 these letters were on the Angels' caps.
24. His 27 saves led the AL in 1967, Minnie _____ .
25. This Angel great set a record by striking out 383 batters in 1973.
27. He replaced Doug Rader as Angel manager in 1991, Buck _____ .
28. He stole 51 bases for the Angels in 1992, Luis _____ .
30. He hit .304 for the Angels back in 1963, outfielder Albie _____ .
33. Angels owner, Gene _____ .
36. One of the Angels' catchers in 1992, John _____ .
37. Angels' bullpen ace in 1992, Joe_____ .

Division Finishes 1983-1992

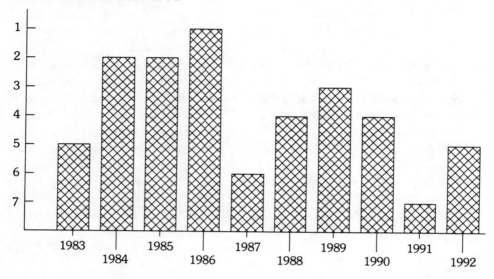

League Leaders 1983-1992

Category	Year	Leader	
Saves	1991	Bryan Harvey	46

1992 Leaders

Category	Player	
Batting Average	Luis Polonia	.286
Home Runs	Gary Gaetti	12
RBI	Junior Felix	72
Stolen Bases	Luis Polonia	51
Doubles	Junior Felix	22
Triples	Junior Felix	5
Runs	Luis Polonia	83
Hits	Luis Polonia	165
Wins	Mark Langston	13
ERA	Jim Abbott	2.77
Strikeouts	Mark Langston	174
Saves	Joe Grahe	21

CHICAGO WHITE SOX

Consisting of twelve teams, the National League was baseball's only major league in the 1890's. There were many problems with the "Big League," several of them traceable to team ownership. Because there were so many teams, there was an imbalance of talent that made the pennant race boring. It wasn't uncommon for the last place club to finish the season sixty games out of first. The problem of talent was underscored by the fact that, in some cases, the same people owned several clubs and would shift players around at will to keep one of their teams always on top of the pennant race.

The owners also had a rule that no player could earn more than $2,400 a year. Needless to say, these problems made for unhappy ball players and many dissatisfied fans.

Charles Comiskey, the owner of a minor league team in St. Paul, along with his friend Ban Johnson, saw an opportunity to start a new league to compete with the National and offer fans a higher quality of baseball. As Comiskey moved his team to Chicago, Johnson organized teams in other cities that wanted and could support a major league team such as Detroit, Baltimore, Milwaukee, Cleveland, Washington, and cities that wanted additional teams such as Boston and Philadelphia. Thus, in 1901 the American League was born.

The Chicago White Sox won the new league's first pennant in 1901. Leading the way was player-manager Clark Griffith who was also the best pitcher on the team. There was no World Series that year, mainly because the National League teams refused to recognize the new league teams as equals. A few years later, fortunately, the dust settled on the baseball wars, and the two leagues agreed to co-exist.

The new league rivalry set the stage for the first intra-city World Series between Chicago's White Sox and Cubs in 1906. The 1906 Cubs dominated the National League like no team ever had, before or since. They won 116 games (still a record) and finished the season 20 games ahead of the second place Giants. By contrast, the White Sox were involved in a fight for the pennant right up to the end.

The Series looked to be a rout for the Cubs. Not only were the Sox weary from the long pennant race, but they had the lowest team batting average in the American League and were called the "Hitless Wonders."

The underdog White Sox pulled off one of the greatest upsets in World Series history, defeating the Cubs in six games. A little known utility infielder named George Rohe suddenly became a World Series hero with two game-winning hits and a Series high .333 batting average.

In 1917, the White Sox again became baseball's World Champions as Comiskey assembled a team full of star players including Shoeless Joe Jackson, Ray Schalk, Eddie Collins, Buck Weaver, and pitchers Eddie Cicotte, Lefty Williams, and Red Faber. In the World Series, they downed the New York Giants, four games to two.

Unfortunately, things were not all right with the team, and Comiskey, even though he helped build the league, nearly tore it down. His heavy-handed dealings and penny-pinching ways so alienated some of his players that they resorted to throwing the 1919 World Series in return for a promise of $10,000 from gamblers.

The White Sox lost the Series to the Cincinnati Reds, and the following year the fix was exposed. The fix became known as the "Black Sox" scandal, and it came close to destroying baseball itself. In 1921, newly appointed Commissioner Kenesaw Mountain Landis expelled for life the eight players involved in the fix, and the game gradually returned to normal.

The White Sox took a lot longer to return to normal. They didn't win their next pennant for forty years. In 1959, the White Sox, led by the aggressive baserunning of Nellie Fox and Luis Aparicio, finally returned to the top of the American League, breaking a string of four consecutive New York Yankee pennants. The team was called the "Go-Go" Sox for their speed, but they also had some hitting punch from Sherm Lollar and Ted Kluszewski and a fine pitching staff headed by Early Wynn, Bob Shaw, Billy Pierce, and bullpen aces Turk Lown and Gerry Staley.

They lost the 1959 World Series to the Los Angeles Dodgers in six games and then hit the skids again through the sixties and seventies. The Sox did not win a division title again until 1983. Led by Cy Young winner LaMarr Hoyt and slugging Rookie of the Year Ron Kittle, the Sox won the AL West by an overwhelming 20 games. Their dominance didn't carry into the playoffs, though. The Baltimore Orioles knocked them out in four games.

In 1990, the White Sox were rejuvenated under Manager Jeff Torborg and became the most improved team in baseball, winning 94 games for the third-best record in the majors. Unfortunately for them, they played in the AL West and finished nine games behind the AL Champion Oakland Athletics.

Although though they fell in the standings in 1991 and 1992, the White Sox still have a strong nucleus and have to be considered a top contender for 1993.

Division Finishes 1983-1992

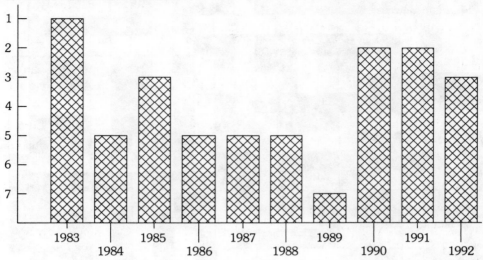

League Leaders 1983-1992

Category	Year	Leader	
Cy Young	1983	LaMarr Hoyt	
Rookie of the Year		Ron Kittle	
Wins		LaMarr Hoyt	21
Winning Pct.		Rich Dotson	.759 (22-7)
Rookie of the Year	1985	Ozzie Guillen	
Saves	1990	Bobby Thigpen	57
Triples	1991	Lance Johnson	13 (T)
Doubles	1992	Frank Thomas	46 (T)
Triples		Lance Johnson	12

1992 Leaders

Category	Player	
Batting Average	Frank Thomas	.323
Home Run	George Bell	25
RBI	Frank Thomas	115
Stolen Bases	Tim Raines	45
Doubles	Frank Thomas	46
Triples	Lance Johnson	12
Runs	Frank Thomas	108
Hits	Frank Thomas	185
Wins	Jack McDowell	20
ERA	Jack McDowell	3.18
Strikeouts	Jack McDowell	178
Saves	Bobby Thigpen	22

44   BASEBALL

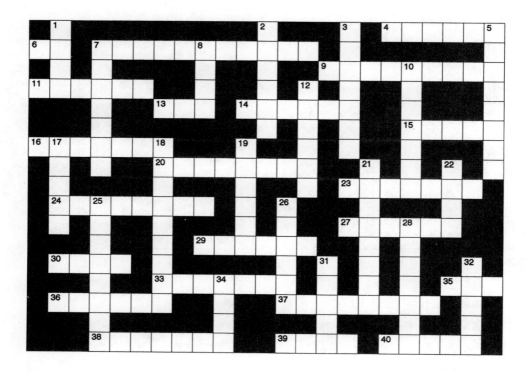

Solution on page 139.

ACROSS

4. One of the Black Sox, first baseman Chick _____ .

6. Chisox slugger who underwent hip surgery in 1992, _____ Jackson.

7. Former NBA great who pitched for the White Sox in the early sixties, Dave _____ .

9. Former University of Miami star, pitcher Alex _____ .

11. Baseball Commissioner who outlawed the Black Sox in 1921.

13. Led the White Sox with a .289 average in the 1983 ALCS, Rudy _____ .

14. Chisox pitching star from the sixties, Gary _____ .

15. Hall of Fame White Sox hurler from 1923 to 1946, Ted _____ .

16. Later known as a baseball clown, he won 20 games for the 1906 World Champion White Sox, Nick _____ .

20. Hall of Fame shortstop for the 1959 AL Champion White Sox.

23. Holds the all time major league single season record for saves with 57.

24. Home of the White Sox, _____ Park.

27. This White Sox pitcher won his 300th game in 1985.

29. This Chicago first baseman belted 32 homers in 1991, Frank _____ .

30. He won 24 and lost 20 for the White Sox in 1973, Wilbur _____ .

33. He won 29 games for the 1919 White Sox, but helped throw the Series, Eddie _____ .

35. Second baseman for the 1959 AL Champion Chisox, Nellie _____ .

36. This left-hander was a White Sox pitching star throughout the fifties, Billy _____ .

37. Away site of the 1959 World Series, the LA _____ .

38. Manager of the 1983 AL West Champion White Sox.

39. This Hall of Famer led the 1959 Sox with 22 victories, Early _____ .

40. He won an amazing total of 40 games for the White Sox in 1908, Hall of Famer Ed _____ .

DOWN

1. Traded to the Cubs for George Bell, Sammy _____ .

2. Third baseman banned from baseball for not reporting what he knew about the 1919 Series fix, Buck _____ .

3. Frustrated manager of the 1919 Sox, Kid _____ .

5. DH for Chicago's 1983 division champs, Greg _____ .

7. They defeated the White Sox in the 1959 World Series.

8. This right-hander won 18 and lost 6 for the 1959 White Sox, Bob _____ .

10. Hall of Fame White Sox shortstop, Luke _____ .

12. This third baseman poked 33 homers in 1971 to lead the league, Bill _____ .

17. Speedy Chicago centerfielder, _____ Johnson.

18. Chisox catcher who knocked in a career high 50 runs in 1992, Ron _____ .

19. Five-time All Star for the White Sox in the fifties, Minnie _____ .

21. _____ Joe Jackson.

22. He won two games in the 1919 World Series in spite of his crooked teammates, Dickie _____ .

25. This Sox pitching ace has won 51 games from 1990 to 1992, Jack_____ .

26. Strikeout artist for the Sox in the late seventies, Ken _____ .

28. Chicago third baseman who knocked in 100 runs in 1991, Robin _____ .

31. This Chisox slugger was the American League's MVP in 1972, Dick _____ .

32. This knuckleballer pitched for the Chisox in 1991 and 1992, Charlie .

34. Former Mexican League star who played for the White Sox in the seventies, Jorge _____ .

# KANSAS CITY ROYALS

Charlie Finley moved the Kansas City Athletics to Oakland after the 1967 season, leaving Kansas City without a team for the first time since 1955. After only a one-year absence, expansion brought a new team to town in 1969, the Royals.

At first, it seemed like a step backward for Kansas City fans to have an established team replaced by an expansion squad, but the Royals quickly erased any memory of the A's in Kansas City fans' minds by achieving success faster than any expansion team before or since.

The success of the Royals can be attributed to their organizational approach. In the expansion draft, they chose mainly young players. They were expected to finish last their first year but won a surprising 69 games to finish fourth.

Kansas City developed their young players into stars, such as Steve Busby, Dennis Leonard, George Brett, Willie Wilson, and Dan Quisenberry. They also made some trades which brought them the talents of Lou Piniella, Amos Otis, John Mayberry, and Hal McRae.

By their third season (1971), the Royals won 85 games to finish in second place. Then, in 1973, they won 88 games to take second again, this time finishing only six games behind the Oakland A's. In 1976, they began a streak of three straight AL West titles, highlighted in 1977 by 102 victories, the most ever by an expansion team at the time. Disappointingly, they were knocked from the playoffs each of those years by the Yankees.

Two of those playoff losses were heartbreakers. In 1976, Chris Chambliss won the pennant for the Yankees with a homer in the bottom of the ninth that broke a 6-6 tie in the fifth and deciding game.

The following year, the Royals took a 3-2 lead into the ninth inning of Game 5 only to witness a Yankee rally wipe them out again.

Finally, in 1980, the Royals beat the Yankees, sweeping them in three games. They won their first American League pennant behind the superb pitching of Leonard, Quisenberry, and Larry Gura. Ironically, the Yankees' manager that year

46

was Dick Howser who eventually led the Royals to their first World Series victory five years later.

The 1980 World Series proved disappointing for first-year manager Jim Frey. The Royals suffered losses in three games in which they had held a lead. Willie Aikens won two games for the Royals with his bat, but the Royals couldn't overcome the Phillies and fell in six games.

The 1985 season turned out to be the Royals' finest. Locked in a tight pennant race with the California Angels, they took three out of four from Gene Mauch's crew in a crucial late-season set and won the division by one game.

The playoff opponent was the AL East champion Blue Jays, who were making their first postseason appearance. The Royals trailed three games to one going into Game 5 when Howser sent Danny Jackson to the mound. The young right-hander responded with a gutsy 2-0 shutout to keep the Royals alive. The series then returned to Toronto for Games 6 and 7, and the rejuvenated Royals swept both for the pennant.

The World Series pitted the Royals against the cross-state St. Louis Cardinals in an all-Missouri event, and the Royals promptly dug themselves in a hole by losing the first two games at home. Twenty-one year old Bret Saberhagen, who led the pitching staff with 20 wins during the regular season, brought the Royals their first victory in Game 3, but John Tudor of the Cards came back with a Game 4 shutout. The Royals were one game from elimination. Once again, Howser called on Jackson who kept his team alive with a 6-1 complete-game victory.

The sixth game of the 1985 World Series still stands as one of the most controversial games of all time. The Cardinals took the field in the bottom of the ninth nursing a one-run lead, three outs away from a championship. The Royals' Jorge Orta grounded a ball to Jack Clark at first base. Clark flipped to Todd Worrell covering the bag but Umpire Don Denkinger called Orta safe.

The television replays showed he was out, and the Cards protested vehemently, but the play stood. With their new life, the Royals pushed across two runs to win the game, then blew the Cards away the next night in Game 7 to take their first World Championship.

Throughout his long career, George Brett has proven himself to be one of baseball's all time greats. He has batted over .300 eleven times, knocked in 100 runs or more four times, and scored over 100 runs four times. He achieved his latest milestone on September 30, 1992 when he got his 3,000th major league hit off the Angel's Tim Fortugno. When Brett's playing days are over, a plaque at Cooperstown most certainly awaits him.

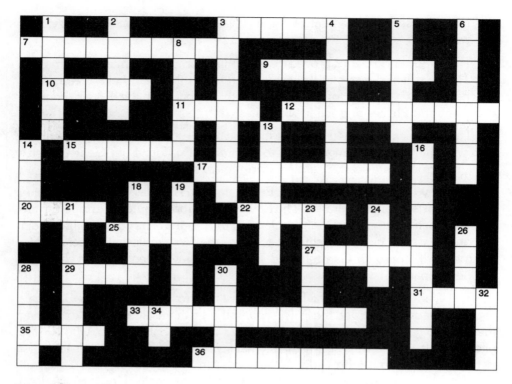

Solution on page 139.

ACROSS

3. Royals' first baseman, former Angel Wally _____ .

7. Royals' catcher who clouted 17 homers in 1992, Mike _____ .

9. KC's first baseman-slugger from the seventies, John _____ .

10. The Royals acquired this pitcher from the Expos in a mid-season 1992 trade, Chris _____ .

11. Bret Saberhagen's bad years.

12. KC's ace reliever since 1989, Jeff___ .

15. Royals' outfielder who batted .312 with 112 RBI's in 1977, Al _____ .

17. Right-hander who won 17 and lost 9 for the 1985 champion Royals, Charlie _____ .

20. The Royals are baseball's only expansion team never to have finished___ .

22. Royals' skipper, Hal _____ .

25. Infielder acquired from the Mets in the Saberhagen trade, Keith _____ .

27. This KC catcher had his best year in 1979, hitting .291 with 20 homers and 112 RBI, Darrell _____ .

29. Free agent flop for the Royals in 1990, _____ Davis.

31. His pinch single in the ninth won Game 6 of the 1985 World Series for the Royals, Dane _____ .

33. KC relief ace of the eighties, Dan __ .

35. Led the 1977 AL West champs in saves and also won 11 games, Doug _____ .

36. Kansas City's major league baseball team before the Royals.

DOWN

1. Royals' manager from 1987 to 1991, John _____ .

2. Royal's all-star shortstop from the seventies, Freddie _____ .

3. Royals' third baseman who hit ten homers and knocked in 75 runs in 1992, Gregg _____ .

4. Royals' GM, Herk _____ .

5. First manager of the expansion Royals in 1969, Joe _____ .

6. Kansas City's team in the old Negro League.

8. First baseman for the 1980 AL champs, Willie _____ .

13. He won 20 and lost 8 for the Royals in 1988, Mark _____ .

14. Royals' catcher from the early seventies, now a New York broadcaster, Fran _____ .

16. Outfielder who hit .301 for the Royals in 1991, Jim _____ .

18. Longtime Royals' utility man, Jamie _____ .

19. Led the '85 Royals in homers with 36, Steve _____ .

21. Royals' backup second baseman Terry _____ .

23. The ace of the Kansas City pitching staff in 1992, Kevin _____ .

24. Left-hand hitting DH for the 1985 World Champion Royals, Jorge _____ .

26. He led the Royals in saves in 1988 with 20, Steve _____ .

28. He pitched no-hitters for the Royals in 1973 and 1974, Steve _____ .

30. The only man to lead his league in batting in three different decades.

32. He posted a 16-4 record for the AL West Champion Royals in 1978, Larry _____ .

34. Shortstop for the 1980 American League champs, _____ Washington.

Division Finishes 1983-1992

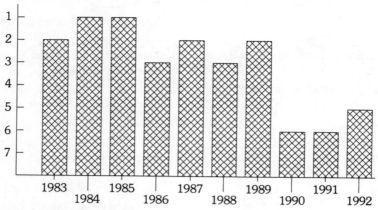

League Leaders 1983-1992

Category	Year	Leader	
Saves	1983	Dan Quisenberry	35
Saves	1984	Dan Quisenberry	45
Cy Young	1985	Bret Saberhagen	
Saves		Dan Quisenberry	37
Triples		Willie Wilson	21
Triples	1987	Willie Wilson	15
Hits		Kevin Seitzer	207 (T)
Triples	1988	Willie Wilson	11 (T)
Cy Young	1989	Bret Saberhagen	
ERA		Bret Saberhagen	2.16
Wins		Bret Saberhagen	23
Winning Pct.		Bret Saberhagen	.793 (23-6)
Batting Average	1990	George Brett	.329
Doubles		George Brett	45 (T)

1992 Leaders

Category	Player	
Batting Average	George Brett	.285
Home Runs	Mike Macfarlane	17
RBI	Gregg Jefferies	75
Stolen Bases	Gregg Jefferies	19
Doubles	Gregg Jefferies	36 (T)
	Wally Joyner	36 (T)
Triples	Brian McRae	5 (T)
	George Brett	5 (T)
Runs	Gregg Jefferies	66 (T)
	Wally Joyner	66 (T)
Hits	Gregg Jefferies	172
Wins	Kevin Appier	15
ERA	Kevin Appier	2.46
Strikeouts	Kevin Appier	150
Saves	Jeff Montgomery	39

MINNESOTA TWINS

The Washington Senators were one of the eight original American League teams. Washington, D.C. had an NL team in the 1880's and 1890's, but the teams were always at or near the cellar. D.C. did not survive the cut when the NL reduced to eight teams in 1900.

The slogan for the Senators was "first in war, first in peace, last in the American League." While this was an appropriate description for several long periods of their history, the Senators were not baseball's worst team. In fact, they had their share of success, and a good number of Hall of Fame players wore the "W" on their caps over the years.

Probably the greatest Senator of all was Walter Johnson. He came up in 1907 and pitched for the Senators for 21 years. He was considered the hardest throwing pitcher of his time, and his outstanding mound efforts carried an otherwise lackluster team throughout most of his career. Not only a great talent, Johnson was also one of baseball's most respected men. He was the perfect role model - a strong, decent man who never argued with umpires or threw at batters.

Johnson, nicknamed "The Big Train," might have gone his entire career without ever appearing in a World Series if the Senators hadn't suddenly put together a strong team in the mid-twenties. In 1924, the managerial duties were handed to a 27-year-old second baseman Bucky Harris who wasted no time in leading his team to the pennant his first year.

Harris' team faced John McGraw's New York Giants in a Series filled with exciting moments. With Game 7 tied 3-3 in the ninth, Johnson was summoned in to pitch. He held New York scoreless through the twelfth. The Senators finally put across a run on a routine ground ball to third that hopped over the third baseman's head after hitting a pebble in the infield. Johnson got his first World Series victory, and Washington took its first-ever title.

The Senators repeated as American League champs in 1925 and, this time, faced the Pittsburgh Pirates in the fall classic. Again, it all came down to a seventh game with Johnson on the mound. But this time the Big Train, now 37, couldn't hold the Pittsburgh bats in check and suffered a 9-7 loss.

The Senators won the pennant again in 1933 by repeating their successful formula of giving the managerial reins to a 27-year-old infielder, Joe Cronin. Cronin led a talented squad of stars into the Series to face the N.Y. Giants but the Senators found themselves overmatched. The Giants won in five games.

A near miss pennant in the war year of 1945 was the only remaining highlight for the Washington club, and, after many years of second-division finishes and poor attendance, owner Calvin Griffith moved the team to Minnesota in 1961.

In the sixties, the Twins assembled a strong team around the hitting of Hall of Famer Harmon Killebrew, Tony Oliva, and Zoilo Versalles, and the pitching of Jim Perry, Jim Kaat and Mudcat Grant. In 1965, the Twins ended the Yankees' string of five pennants and faced off against the Dodgers in the World Series. The series went to seven games, but the Twins lost.

Hall of Famer Rod Carew joined the Twins in 1967 and won the Rookie of the Year Award. He led the Twins to division titles in 1969 and 1970, but they couldn't get past the tough Orioles.

Carew excited Twins fans throughout the seventies. In 1977, Carew hit .388, the highest batting average since Ted Williams' .406 in 1941. Overall, he won seven batting titles with the Twins. But, with the advent of free agency, the Twins found themselves unable to compete financially. They lost Carew and outfielder Lyman Bostock and entered a period of decline.

New ownership in the eighties gave the Twins the finances to hold on to some of their young stars. Kirby Puckett, Kent Hrbek, Frank Viola, and Gary Gaetti led a surprising Twins team into the 1987 World Series against the St. Louis Cardinals. The Twins won all four of their home games and captured their first World Championship since moving to Minnesota.

After finishing in last place in 1990, the Twins won the AL pennant in 1991, and the right to meet the Atlanta Braves in the World Series. The Braves, who also finished last the year before, joined the Twins in baseball's only worst-to-first Series.

And what a series it was! Packed with thrills, clutch hitting, great fielding plays, and, above all, excellent pitching, it has been called the most dramatic World Series of all time.

Five of the seven games were decided by one run, four decided in the last at-bat, and three games, including the nail-biting sixth and seventh games, went into extra innings. Kirby Puckett's eleventh inning homer won game 6 for the Twins, and Jack Morris's ten-inning shutout in Game 7 gave the Twins their second World Championship in five years.

Division Finishes 1983-1992

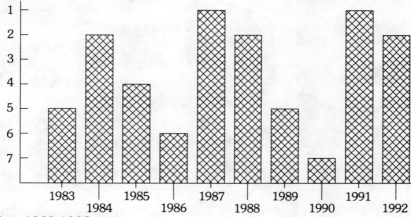

Leaders 1983-1992

Category	Year	Leader	
Strikeouts	1985	Bert Blyleven *	206
Hits	1987	Kirby Puckett	207
Cy Young	1988	Frank Viola	
ERA		Allan Anderson	2.45
Wins		Frank Viola	24
Winning Pct.		Frank Viola	.774 (24-7)
Hits		Kirby Puckett	234
Batting Average	1989	Kirby Puckett	.339
Hits		Kirby Puckett	215
Rookie of the Year	1991	Chuck Knoblauch	
Wins		Scott Erickson	20 (T)
Winning Pct.		Scott Erickson	.714 (20-8)
Hits	1992	Kirby Puckett	210

* Also pitched for Cleveland in 1985.

1992 Leaders

Category	Leader	
Batting Average	Kirby Puckett	.329
Home Runs	Kirby Puckett	19
RBI	Kirby Puckett	110
Stolen Bases	Chuck Knoblauch	34
Doubles	Kirby Puckett	38
Triples	Chuck Knoblauch	6 (T)
	Shane Mack	6 (T)
Runs	Chuck Knoblauch	104 (T)
	Kirby Puckett	104 (T)
Hits	Kirby Puckett	210
Wins	John Smiley	16 (T)
	Kevin Tapani	16 (T)
ERA	John Smiley	3.21
Strikouts	John Smiley	163
Saves	Rick Aguilera	41

Solution on page 139.

ACROSS

3. This third baseman for the Senators during the fifties ranks among the all-time leaders in walks, Eddie _____ .

6. He won 25 games for the 1966 Twins, Jim _____ .

9. Hall of Famer who retired in 1975 with 573 home runs.

11. This outfielder ended his Hall of Fame career in 1934 with a total of 2,987 hits, Sam _____ .

12. All Star catcher for the Twins in 1988, Tim _____ .

13. Twins' 1991 ALCS opponent.

14. His three run homer won Game 1 of the 1991 World Series for the Twins, shortstop Greg _____ .

16. He managed the Twins to the 1965 AL pennant, Sam _____ .

18. This Washington first baseman won batting titles in 1946 and 1953, Mickey _____ .

20. The Twins have not _____ a home World Series game since 1965.

23. Top AL reliever in 1969 and 1970, Ron _____ .

25. Catcher for the 1965 AL champion Twins, Earl _____ .

27. He had a 31-game hitting streak in 1980, Ken _____ .

30. This left-handed journeyman reliever picked up the win in Game 6 of the 1987 World Series, Dan _____ .

31. First baseman for the 1965 Twins, Don _____ .

34. One of the Twin Cities.

35. Appleton, Minn. native who won 20 games for the Twins in 1979, Jerry _____ .

36. Twins' superstar _____ Puckett.

37. Home of the Twins, the _____ Dome.
38. Left-handed pitcher traded to the Phillies after the 1992 season, David ___ .
39. Twin reserve who got the winning RBI in the tenth inning of Game 7 of the 1991 World Series, Gene _____ .

DOWN

1. His best year as a Twin was 1988 when he won 24 and lost 7.
2. 1965 American League MVP, Zoilo _____ .
4. He won the AL batting crown in 1964, 1965 and 1971, Tony _____ .
5. They called Walter Johnson the Big _____ .
6. Twins' skipper since 1986, Tom _____ .
7. Twins' stopper with 40-plus saves in 1991 and 1992, Rick _____ .
8. The Twins' 1987 World Series opponent.
10. The Twins' 1991 World Series opponent.
14. Hall of Fame outfielder who starred in three World Series for Washington, Goose _____ .

15. Second baseman for the 1991 World Champs, Chuck _____ .
16. 1991 World Series MVP.
17. Twins' third baseman who became AL Rookie of the Year in 1979, John _____ .
19. This right-hander went 16-9 for the 1991 World Champion Twins, Kevin _____ .
21. Power hitting shortstop for the Twins in the late 1970's, Roy _____ .
22. Third baseman for the 1991 World Champs, Mike _____ .
24. Backup catcher for the 1991 World Champs, Junior _____ .
26. Twins' 1965 World Series opponents.
28. Twins' first baseman since 1981.
29. Player-manager of the 1933 AL champion Senators, Joe _____ .
32. He led the American League in doubles in 1970, _____ Tovar.
33. Twins' slugger from the sixties, _____ Allison.

# OAKLAND ATHLETICS

In the early 1950's, baseball entered an era of franchise shifts, marking the first changes to the grand old game's makeup since the turn of the century. After World War II, baseball, like all of America, experienced boom years. Major league attendance in 1946, the first year after the war, reached new heights and attendance marks remained high into the fifties. Several cities had two major league teams in those days, but these cities soon found that the new prosperity did not extend to both hometown teams. Many of the "second" teams moved on to greener (as in money) pastures. This is what happened in Boston, St. Louis, and Philadelphia.

In Philadelphia, the American League Athletics had owned the town for years, but the National League Phillies had captured the city's imagination with an exciting pennant victory in 1950. They were a young team and were known as the "Whiz Kids." Their future looked bright while the once awesome A's were mired in decline.

With the Phillies now the city's favorites, their successes overshadowing the A's both on the field and at the turnstiles, the A's decided to move to Kansas City for the 1955 season. As a result, Philadelphia lost its greatest team, one that had won five World Championships and would win four more for a new city.

In the first half of this century, Philadelphia baseball and Connie Mack were synonymous. Mr. Mack was the team's owner and manager for 50 years, finally retiring in 1950 at the age of 88.

Under Mack, the A's enjoyed two periods during which they dominated baseball. The first period was between 1910 and 1914. With a pitching staff led by Chief Bender, Eddie Plank and Jack Coombs, and Hall of Famers Eddie Collins and Home Run Baker spearheading Mack's $100,000 infield, the club won four pennants and three World Series titles. Their only postseason loss came in 1914 when they were stunned, four games to none, by the "Miracle Braves" of Boston.

The team was soon dismantled as a new baseball league, the Federal League, was formed and signed away some of Mack's stars. Mack was compelled to sell off others to avoid a bidding war.

The A's returned to prominence in 1929. Between 1929 and 1931, the Philadelphians won three straight American league pennants and two World Championships at a time when the Ruth-Gehrig Yankees were in their heyday. This crop of Mackmen was led by Lefty Grove, considered by some to be the greatest pitcher of all time, and Hall of Famers Mickey Cochrane, Al Simmons and Jimmie Foxx.

This team was also broken up by Mack for financial reasons, and the remainder of the team's stay in Philadelphia was largely unsuccessful.

The A's played in Kansas City from 1955 to 1967 before moving again, this time to Oakland. Their KC stay was notable both for the antics of their controversial new owner Charles Finley and for the fact that, in the mid-sixties, the KC teams served as an assembly plant for the great Oakland Athletics teams of the seventies.

In 1971, the A's completed their rise to the top of the standings, winning the AL West championship with a record of 101-60. Dick Williams, who piloted the 1967 Boston Red Sox to their "Impossible Dream" season, was at the helm of a team boasting a long list of talented stars, such as Reggie Jackson, Joe Rudi, Bert Campaneris, Sal Bando, Catfish Hunter and Vida Blue.

The A's followed in 1972-74 with three straight World Championships, displaying a dominance not seen in baseball since Casey Stengel's Yankees of the fifties. No one will ever know how long this team could have stayed on top, because free agency broke this great team up. Finley refused to pay the high salaries being offered by other owners.

Oakland surprised everyone in the strike year of 1981 when new manager Billy Martin breathed new life into the team with his exciting brand of baseball known as "Billyball." The A's took the AL West crown that year but lost to the Yankees in the playoffs.

Billyball turned out to be a one-year phenomenon, and the A's lapsed into a rebuilding period. Their hard work paid off in 1988 when the Athletics again reeled off three straight pennants (1988-1990).They were led by the pitching of Dave Stewart and Bob Welch, and the hitting of Rickey Henderson and the "Bash Brothers," Jose Canseco and Mark McGwire. The high point of this period was the A's 4-0 sweep of the Giants in the 1989 World Series.

Manager Tony LaRussa displayed his managerial genius one more time in 1992, as he led an injury-ridden A's team to yet another American League West title. Dennis Eckersley was virtually unbeatable all year in relief with a 7-1 record and 51 saves, earning him both the AL MVP and Cy Young awards, but the Blue Jays took the A's in a hard-fought playoff series, four games to two.

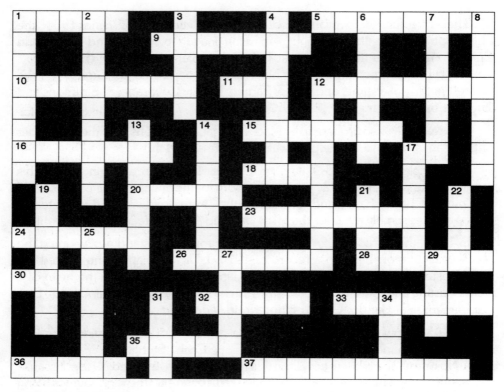

Solution on page 140.

ACROSS

1. He won 27 while losing only 6 for the 1990 A's, Bob _____ .

5. This Hall of fame catcher was the backbone of the great A's teams of 1929-1931, Mickey _____ .

9. Turn-of-the-century strikeout king, Rube _____ .

10. Left-handed relief specialist for the A's in the '60's and '70's, Paul _____ .

11. He caught for the Kansas City A's but achieved his greatest fame as a batting coach, Charlie _____ .

12. This right-hander won 21 and lost 13 for the 1973 World Champion A's, Ken _____ .

15. In the early sixties, Charlie Finley shortened the right field fence in Kansas City and called it the _____ porch.

16. This A's hurler led the American League in ERA in the strike year of 1981, Steve _____ .

17. Batting average (abbrev.).

18. This A's pitcher was the American League MVP in 1971.

20. The A's traded this shortstop to the Florida Marlins during the 1992 expansion draft, Walt _____ .

23. This third baseman batted .438 in the 1989 World Series sweep of San Francisco, Carney _____ .

24. He began a long, distinguished career as a centerfielder with Connie Mack's A's in 1929, Doc _____ .

26. He never hit more than 12 in a season, but this A's third baseman was always known as _____ Baker.

28. He posted a 22-9 record for Oakland in 1980, Mike _____ .

30. Rightfielder for the 1929-1931 Philadelphia A's, _____ Miller.

32. Catcher for the 1973 and 1974 World Champion A's, Ray _____ .

33. This Hall of Famer was known as "Bucketfoot" for his unusual batting stance, Al _____ .

35. Pitching ace for the A's of 1929-1931, Lefty _____ .

36. First baseman for the Kansas City A's in the fifties, Vic _____ .

37. Shortstop for the 1972-1974 World Champion A's, Bert _____ .

DOWN

1. Manager of the 1972 and 1973 World Champion A's, Dick _____ .

2. The A's opponents in the 1930 and 1931 World Series.

3. Covered third base for Oakland from 1968 to 1976, Sal _____ .

4. A rookie with the 1974 World Champion A's, he went on to a long major league career, _____ Washington.

6. Second baseman for Connie Mack's $100,000 infield, Hall of Famer Eddie _____ .

7. Oakland _____ County Coliseum.

8. Right-handed pitching ace on the 1929-1931 A's teams, George _____ .

12. Baseball's all-time stolen base leader.

13. Twenty-game winner for Oakland from 1987 to 1990, Dave _____ .

14. He blasted 42 homers and 124 RBI for the A's in 1988.

17. Standout pitcher for the Philadelphia A's from 1903 to 1914, Chief _____ .

19. Philadelphia A's slugger from the early fifties, Gus _____ .

21. Blue _____ Odom.

22. Clutch hitter for the A's in the seventies, Joe _____ .

25. After hitting only .201 in 1991, this Oakland slugger bounced back in 1992 with one of his best seasons ever.

27. This right-hander went 19-11 for the 1989 A's including two wins in their World Series sweep, Mike _____ .

29. A's catcher from the 1960's, Phil _____ .

31. His best year for the KC A's was 1958 when he blasted 38 homers and 104 RBI, Bob _____ .

34. Charlie Finley's mascot for the Kansas City A's.

Division Finishes 1983-1992

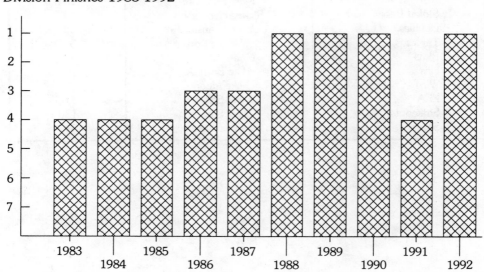

League Leaders 1983-1992

Category	Year	Leader	
Stolen Bases	1983	Rickey Henderson	108
Stolen Bases	1984	Rickey Henderson	66
Rookie of the Year	1986	Jose Canseco	
Rookie of the Year	1987	Mark McGwire	
Home Runs		Mark McGwire	49
Wins		Dave Stewart	20 (T)
MVP	1988	Jose Canseco	
Rookie of the Year		Walt Weiss	
Home Runs		Jose Canseco	42
RBI		Jose Canseco	124
Saves		Dennis Eckersley	45
Stolen Bases	1989	Rickey Henderson *	77
Runs		Rickey Henderson *	113 (T)
MVP	1990	Rickey Henderson	
Cy Young		Bob Welch	
Wins		Bob Welch	27
Winning Pct.		Bob Welch	.818 (27-6)
Stolen Bases		Rickey Henderson	65
Runs		Rickey Henderson	119
Home Runs	1991	Jose Canseco	44 (T)
Stolen Bases		Rickey Henderson	58
Cy Young	1992	Dennis Eckersley	
MVP		Dennis Eckersley	
Saves		Dennis Eckersley	51

* Also played for the New York Yankees in 1989.

1992 Leaders

Category	Player	
Batting Average	Mike Bordick	.300
Home Runs	Mark McGwire	42
RBI	Mark McGwire	104
Stolen Bases	Rickey Henderson	48
Doubles	Carney Lansford	30
Triples	Willie Wilson	5
Runs	Mark McGwire	87
Hits	Mike Bordick	151
Wins	Mike Moore	17
ERA	Dave Stewart	3.66
Strikeouts	Dave Stewart	130
Saves	Dennis Eckersley	51

SEATTLE MARINERS

Back in 1968, the expansion Seattle Pilots drafted a young outfielder from the Cleveland Indians named Lou Piniella. Piniella never settled in Seattle then, because he was traded before the start of the season. Twenty-four years later, he's finally making the move to Seattle to become manager of the Mariners for 1993.

If there were ever a team with no place to go but up, it would be Seattle. The Mariners finished the 1992 season with a 64-98 record, the same mark posted by the expansion Mariners in their first season of 1977.

Success has eluded the Mariners so far. They have never finished higher than fourth place. In fact, only once have they finished above .500. However, they are not alone in their futility when compared with the first sixteen years of some of the charter members of modern-day baseball:

Team	Dates	Winning Pct.
Reds	1901-1916	.464
Dodgers	1901-1916	.447
Mariners	1977-1992	.427
Cardinals	1901-1916	.408

As everyone knows, the Dodgers, Cardinals and Reds have all gone on to great success. It just took some time to get their franchises in gear. The comparison with the Cardinals is particularly striking, since Hall of Fame executive Branch Rickey was hired in 1917 and promptly began the process of molding the Cards into championship material. The Mariners began 1993 with numerous management changes, including new ownership, and hope to produce similar winning results.

Until the change happens, the Mariners have the distinction of being one of only two expansion clubs never to have won even a division title (the Texas Rangers are the other).

Things got off on the wrong foot for major league baseball in Seattle in 1969, when the expansion Seattle Pilots joined the American League. Conditions at Sicks' Stadium, the Pilots' home park, quickly became a cause of friction between club management and city leaders.

By season's end, the situation was so bad that the team couldn't help but notice that several other cities were dying for the chance to call a major league team their own. These cities included Milwaukee, Toronto, and Dallas-Fort Worth. After only one season in Seattle, the team fled to Milwaukee to become the Brewers.

Seattle, stung by this sudden move, found itself building a domed stadium with no team to play in it. They threatened the American League with a lawsuit. This sticky situation proved to be the impetus for the AL's hasty expansion in 1977, which brought baseball back to the Great Northwest in the form of the Mariners.

Former Red Sox manager Darrell Johnson managed the Mariners through their early seasons, and the team performed slightly better that the other AL expansion entry, the Toronto Blue Jays. But while the Jays found the formula to become one of the top American League teams by the mid-eighties, the M's never found a way to step to the next level.

Part of the reason for this was the constant managerial changes made by Owner George Argyros in the eighties. During the time, Maury Wills, Rene Lachemann, Del Crandall, Chuck Cottier, and Dick Williams all passed through the Seattle revolving door.

Another reason for the M's lack of success was its inability to hold on to some of its young stars such as Floyd Bannister, Danny Tartabull, Mark Langston and Mike Moore. The loss of players with potential caused the team to continously seem to be starting from scratch.

Seattle fans have had some things to cheer about though. Gaylord Perry pitched his 300th victory in 1982. Alvin Davis thrilled Seattle fans with his remarkable Rookie of the Year Performance in 1984. Randy Johnson threw a no-hitter in 1990 and led the league in strikeouts in 1992. Dave Fleming had a tremendous start in 1992, and Ken Griffey, Jr. has put in consistently great performances for Seattle.

The 1991 season was the best ever for the Mariners. They finished with an 83-79 record, their first ever winning season. It was just their luck, however, that it would only get them fifth place as the entire AL West finished .500 or better that year.

Despite threats to move the team or sell to Japanese buyers, Seattle fans continue to come out to the Kingdome in record numbers, over two million in 1991. New management, which includes Japanese investors, have sent signals that they are serious about improving the team.

So with sixteen seasons under their belts, the Mariners enter 1993 with new leadership, a new direction, and still, no place to go but up.

Division Finishes 1983-1992

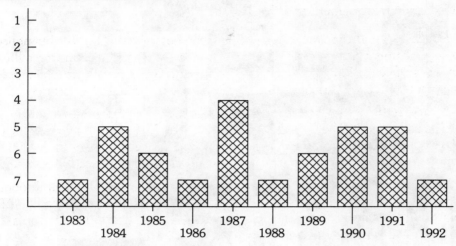

League Leaders 1983-1992

Category	Year	Leader	
Rookie of the Year	1984	Alvin Davis	
Strikeouts		Mark Langston	204
Strikeouts	1986	Mark Langston	245
Strikeouts	1987	Mark Langston	262
Stolen Bases		Harold Reynolds	60
Triples	1988	Harold Reynolds	11 (T)
Batting Average	1992	Edgar Martinez	.343
Strikeouts		Randy Johnson	241
Doubles		Edgar Martinez	46 (T)

1992 Leaders

Category	Player	
Batting Average	Edgar Martinez	.343
Home Runs	Ken Griffey, Jr.	27
RBI	Ken Griffey, Jr.	103
Stolen Bases	Henry Cotto	23
Doubles	Edgar Martinez	46
Triples	Ken Griffey, Jr.	4 (T)
	Omar Vizquel	4 (T)
Runs	Edgar Martinez	100
Hits	Edgar Martinez	181
Wins	Dave Fleming	17
ERA	Dave Fleming	3.39
Strikeouts	Randy Johnson	241
Saves	Mike Schooler	13

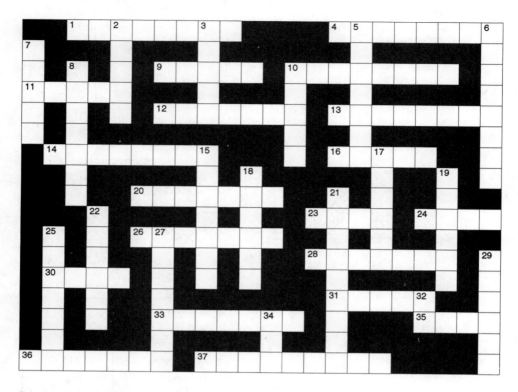

Solution on page 140.

ACROSS

1. The Mariners' home ballpark.

4. He racked up 33 saves for the M's in 1989, Mike _____ .

9. He reached the majors in 1992 to become baseball's first third-generation ballplayer, Bret _____ .

10. Edgar or Tino.

11. He shared the catching duties with Lance Parrish in 1992, Dave _____ .

12. This Seattle third baseman knocked in 107 runs in 1986, Jim _____ .

13. Video game company owned by the new majority owner of the Mariners.

14. Veteran manager who led the M's from 1986 to 1988, Dick _____ .

16. Former Twin who played left field for the expansion M's in 1977, Steve___ .

20. This right-hander won 12 games for Seattle in 1991, Rich _____ .

23. He led the Mariners in wins (10) and saves (11) back in 1978, Enrique ___ .

24. This left-hander was the M's workhorse out of the bullpen in 1992, Russ ___ .

26. He owned the Mariners from 1981 to 1989, George _____ .

28. Acquired from the Yankees, this pitcher became a mainstay on the Seattle staff in the early eighties, Jim___ .

30. This former Pirate DHed for the Mariners from 1981 to 1983, Richie ___ .

31. This Seattle outfielder batted .305 while seeing limited duty in 1991, Henry _____ .

33. Power hitting outfielder for the expansion M's, _____ Jones.

35. This shortstop was traded to the Red Sox for the 1986 stretch drive, Spike _____ .

36. This pitching great struck out 20 Mariners in a 1986 game.

37. This Mariner hurler struck out 209 batters in 1982 to lead the American League, Floyd _____ .

DOWN

2. Mariner reliever in the mid-eighties, Edwin _____ .

3. His best year as a Mariner was 1985 when he posted a 17-10 record, Mike _____ .

5. He managed the Mariners in 1985, Chuck _____ .

6. This Seattle second baseman hit .300 in 1989, Harold _____ .

7. He blasted 27 homers and 116 RBI as a Mariner rookie in 1984, Alvin ____ .

8. Rookie pitching sensation for the M's in 1992, Dave _____ .

10. He played first base for the 1977 expansion Mariners and knocked in 90 runs, tying Leroy Stanton for the team lead, Dan _____ .

15. Mariner owner who sold the team in 1992, Jeff _____ .

17. He led the Seattle staff with 12 wins in their inaugural season of 1977, Glenn _____ .

18. Seattle's 1969 major league team.

19. This Seattle reliever led the staff in saves in 1980 and 1981, Shane ____ .

21. He pitched for the Mariners in their first season (1977) and for the Oakland A's in the 1992 ALCS, Rick ____ .

22. This right-hander posted an 18-9 record for the Mariners in 1990, Erik _____ .

25. This Seattle shortstop hit a career high .294 in 1992, Omar _____ .

27. This outfielder led the Mariners' offense in 1978 with 22 homers, 92 runs batted in and a .301 average, Leon _____ .

29. This outfielder blasted 25 homers for the M's in 1992, Jay _____ .

32. Jeffrey Leonard wore this number.

34. Home _____ .

# TEXAS RANGERS

Keeping a baseball team in Washington D.C. was, for many years, considered a necessity by the "Lords of Baseball."

The reason for this dates back to 1922, when a decision by the U.S. Supreme Court effectively granted major league baseball an exemption from federal antitrust regulations. This made it possible for the owners to use the reserve clause to keep players' salaries down and to keep players tied to one team for their entire careers.

To please the Washington legislators , who held the power to review baseball's exemption, a team was kept in D.C. until 1971, despite conditions that might have warranted a franchise move had it been located in any other city.

The Washington Senators were a charter member of the American League. In the 1950's, owner Calvin Griffith sought to move the team to Minneapolis. Other owners resisted the move for fear of upsetting Congress.

When the American League approved modern baseball's first-ever expansion in 1961, the Senators were permitted to move to Minnesota to become the Twins, and Washington was granted one of the expansion franchises, to be known as — that's right — the Senators.

If this move was confusing to baseball fans, imagine the dilemma of pitchers Hal Woodeshick and Rudy Hernandez who were selected by the new Senators in the expansion draft from the old Senators. When they returned to Griffith Stadium for the 1961 season, they found their old team was gone and replaced by an entirely new one.

The new Senators are the forerunners of today's Texas Rangers.

The new Senators' eleven year stay in Washington was largely unsuccessful. They lost 100 or more games in each of their first four seasons. In 1963, they made an unusual trade with the New York Mets, shipping Jimmy Piersall off to the Polo Grounds in exchange for Gil Hodges.

Hodges had reached the end of the line as a player, but the Senators had acquired him to be their manager. Hodges managed the team until 1967, when he was traded back to the Mets. During Hodges' tenure as manager, he guided the Senators toward respectability with win totals of 71, 72 and 76. The latter was good enough for a sixth place tie in 1967.

In 1969, the Senators made big headlines by signing the immortal Ted Williams as their new manager. The move paid off brilliantly as Williams guided the team to its first-ever winning season, an 86-76 mark that earned the Senators fourth place in the American League East.

Unfortunately, Williams' Senators failed to improve upon its '69 mark. He managed through 1972, but his teams never did as well again.

In 1972, the team moved to Arlington, Texas, changing their name to the Texas Rangers. Their first two seasons in their new surroundings were reminiscent of their Senator days as they fell back to the 100-loss level, but in 1974 things changed.

An off-season trade brought future Hall of Famer Ferguson Jenkins to Texas, and he responded with 25 wins in his first Ranger season. Young outfielder Jeff Burroughs also had an outstanding year and became the American league MVP. First-year manager Billy Martin's trademark exciting brand of baseball had Texas fans cheering the Rangers on to their best year yet, a second place finish, just five games behind the eventual World Champion Oakland A's .

The season of 1977 proved to be another good year for the Rangers despite a bad start. Infielder Len Randle beat up Manager Frank Lucchesi during spring training because Randle did not like the idea that he was benched. By mid-season, both Randle and Lucchesi were gone. The Rangers went on to enjoy their best season ever. Doyle Alexander, Gaylord Perry and Bert Blyleven spearheaded a strong pitching staff, and Toby Harrah and Mike Hargrove fueled the offense. The Rangers finished the season with a 94-68 record, but again they ended up in second place, eight games behind the Royals.

As of 1992, the Rangers are one of only two teams (Seattle Mariners, the other) that have never won either a division title or a pennant. Still, Texas has managed to work its way into the spotlight in recent years. The Rangers signed free agent Nolan Ryan after the 1988 season, and the native Texan became an instant hero. Ryan, apparently an ageless wonder, amazes the baseball world each season with record breaking performances. While in Texas, Ryan has led the league in strike-outs twice and pitched his record sixth and seventh no-hitters. Ryan struck out his 5,000th batter while in Texas uniform.

In 1992, the Rangers brought Jose Canseco to Texas in exchange for Ruben Sierra, Jeff Russell, and Bobby Witt. The trade was prompted by the fact that Sierra's contract was expiring at the end of the season, and the Ranger's did not feel that they could re-sign him. The trade has come to symbolize the new philosophy of baseball management in the era of high-priced superstars and free agents.

Canseco's presence bolsters an already potent offensive lineup, joining sluggers Juan Gonzalez and Dean Palmer and perennial batting title contenders Julio Franco and Rafael Palmeiro.

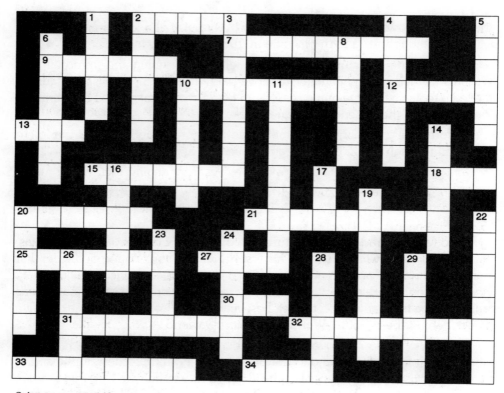

Solution on page 140.

ACROSS

2. This well-traveled outfielder DHed for the Rangers in 1980 and batted .300, Rusty _____ .

7. The Rangers' Gold Glove catcher, Ivan _____ .

9. This Texas third baseman blasted 26 homers in 1992, Dean _____ .

10. Homer and RBI leader for the Rangers in 1991 and 1992, Juan _____ .

12. The Senators' bullpen ace of the sixties, Ron _____ .

13. 1969 AL Manager of the Year, _____ Williams.

15. His 2.40 ERA led the American League in 1961 for the expansion Senators, Dick _____ .

18. The Senators' home ballpark in the sixties.

20. He blasted 48 homers in 1969 for the Senators, Frank _____ .

21. This Senator rookie was the starting pitcher in the 1962 All Star Game, Dave _____ .

25. He notched 30 saves for the Rangers in 1991, Jeff _____ .

27. Bullpen ace for the Rangers in 1979 with a 13-5 record and 29 saves, Jim _____ .

30. First baseman on some bad Senator teams of the 1960's, Dick _____ .

31. Batted .322 for the Rangers in 1991, Rafael _____ .

32. Manager of the Rangers from 1985 to 1992.

33. Third baseman traded to the Pirates for the 1991 stretch drive, Steve _____ .

34. Set a Ranger record with 301 strike-outs in 1989.

DOWN

1. American League batting leader in 1991 with a .341 average, _____ Franco.

2. Outfielder traded to Oakland in the Canseco deal.

3. Shortstop for the Senators in the sixties, Eddie _____ .

4. Catfish Hunter won the 1974 Cy Young Award but this Ranger ace had an identical 25-12 record that year.

5. This left-hander led Texas in saves in 1990 with 15, Kenny _____ .

6. He hit 30 home runs and batted .278 for the 1969 Senators, Mike _____ .

8. He won 16 and lost 11 for the Rangers in 1992, Jose _____ .

10. Rangers' General manager and former outfielder, Tom _____ .

11. The Rangers call this Texas city home.

14. At age 20, he led Ranger pitchers in strikeouts in 1986 with 189, Ed _____ .

16. Ranger first baseman from 1983 to 1988, Pete _____ .

17. He fizzled as a late-season acquisition for the Rangers in 1991, Oil _____ Boyd.

19. He managed the Rangers in 1979 and 1980, Pat _____ .

20. Hard hitting Ranger shortstop from the 1970's Toby _____ .

22. Stand-out defensive catcher for the Rangers in the seventies and eighties, Jim _____ .

23. Number one Ranger draft pick in 1973 who went right to the majors, pitcher David _____ .

24. The first manager of the expansion Senators in 1961, Mickey _____ .

26. This Texas outfielder from the early eighties later became a baseball broadcaster, Billy _____ .

28. He won 31 games for the Tigers in 1968, but he lost 22 for the Senators in 1971, Denny _____ .

29. Frank Lucchesi replaced him as Ranger manager in 1975, Billy _____ .

Division Finishes 1983-1992

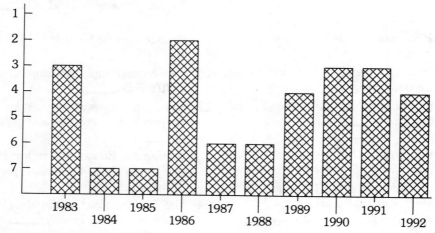

League Leaders 1983-1992

Category	Year	Leader	
ERA	1983	Rick Honeycutt	2.42
RBI	1989	Ruben Sierra	119
Strikeouts		Nolan Ryan	301
Saves		Jeff Russell	38
Triples		Ruben Sierra	14
Strikeouts	1990	Nolan Ryan	232
Hits		Rafael Palmeiro	191
Batting Average	1991	Julio Franco	.341
Doubles		Rafael Palmeiro	49
Home Runs	1992	Juan Gonzalez	43
Wins		Kevin Brown	21 (T)

1992 Leaders

Category	Player	
Batting Average	Rafael Palmeiro	.268
Home Runs	Juan Gonzalez	43
RBI	Juan Gonzalez	109
Stolen Bases	Jeff Huson	18
Doubles	Kevin Reimer	32
Triples	Ruben Sierra	6
Runs	Juan Gonzalez	77
Hits	Rafael Palmeiro	163
Wins	Kevin Brown	21
ERA	Kevin Brown	3.32
Strikeouts	Jose Guzman	179
Saves	Jeff Russell	28

CHICAGO CUBS

The Chicago White Stockings were one of the charter members of the National League when the league began in 1876. This team, later to be known as the Cubs, is baseball's oldest single-city franchise.

In 1876, they won the National League's first pennant, led by the performances of pitcher Al Spalding and third baseman Cap Anson. Spalding soon retired to start the sporting goods business that bears his name, and Anson became player-manager a few years later, continuing as a regular until 1897, when he retired after a 27-year career. While he played, Anson was one of baseball's biggest stars.

Soon after the turn of the century, the Cubs became one of the most dominant teams in baseball, winning four pennants between 1906 and 1910. Their success can be attributed in part to the strong pitching staff, led by Hall of Famer Mordecai "Three Finger" Brown, Ed Reulbach and Orvie Overall. Brown, so nicknamed because he lost one finger and the use of another in a childhood accident, turned his condition to his advantage as a pitcher as it gave him an unusually effective pitching grip.

The Cub infield consisted of Harry Steinfeldt at third, and the immortal double play combination of Tinker to Evers to Chance, who were immortalized in the popular poem by Franklin P. Adams. In fact, all three entered the Hall of Fame together in 1946.

The 1906, the Cubs set a record with 116 regular season wins but were upset in the World Series by their crosstown rivals "The Hitless Wonder" White Sox. They bounced back to win back-to-back world championships in 1907 and 1908, defeating Ty Cobb and the Detroit Tigers both times. They won another pennant in 1910 but fell to Connie Mack's Philadelphia Athletics in the World Series.

Starting in 1929, the Cubs began a pattern of winning a pennant once every three years. They took the National League title in 1929, 1932, 1935, and 1938.

In 1929, less than a week after the great stock market crash, the Cubs once again met the Philadelphia A's in the World Series and, again, lost, four games to one. The 1932 Series pitted the Cubs against the Yankees who were led by Ruth,

Gehrig and company. The Cubs suffered a four game sweep at the hands of the pinstripers and became embroiled for all time in the controversy of whether Babe Ruth really "called his shot" in Game 3.

The 1935 pennant winning Cubs fell victim to the Tigers in the Series as the latter won their first championship. Then in 1938, the Chicagoans fell in four to the Yankees. They may have spent themselves in a hard fought pennant race with the Pirates, one which was capped by player-manager Gabby Hartnett's late season game-winning homer into the Wrigley Field darkness.

In 1945, the Cubs again were crowned National League champions but were defeated in the Series by Detroit again, this time taking the Tigers to seven games. This remains the Cubs' last appearance in the fall classic.

Though the Cubs generally fielded poor teams during the fifties, they had a few highlights, such as Hank Sauer's MVP year in 1952 and the emergence of Ernie Banks as one of the game's greats. Banks won back to back MVP awards in 1958 and 1959, and his genial personality made him the most popular Cub ever. Indeed, he is still known today as "Mr. Cub."

The team's losing ways continued in the 1960's, but they began to put together a group of very solid ballplayers. Among these were future Hall of Famers Banks, Billy Williams and Ferguson Jenkins, plus an infield of Ron Santo, Don Kessinger and Glenn Beckert, and pitchers Ken Holtzman and Bill Hands.

It all seemed to come together for the Cubs in 1969, when they looked as though they might run away with the NL East title. Unfortunately for them, their gradual rise to power was suddenly eclipsed by the meteoric rise of the formerly hapless Mets. The Cubs slumped; the Mets went on to win the World Series, and the long drought continued.

Possibly the Cub's greatest disappointment came in 1984 when they again locked horns with the Mets in a pennant race. This time the Cubs soundly knocked the Mets out of the race in head-on encounters on their way to their first ever division title. In the playoffs, they faced the Padres, who, like the 1969 Mets, had never won anything before. The Cubs won the first two games of the best of five series, then traveled to San Diego needing only one win out of three for the pennant. They lost all three games.

When the 1989 season began, the Cubs weren't expected to contend but they won the division handily under manager Don Zimmer. Their infield was solid with Ryne Sandberg, Shawon Dunston and Mark Grace. The outfield featured Andre Dawson in right, and two rookie phenoms, Dwight Smith and Jerome Walton. And the pitching staff was bolstered by a super relief performance by "Wild Thing" Mitch Williams. Once again, however, they met with defeat in the NLCS, this time at the hands of the Giants.

Division Finishes 1983-1992

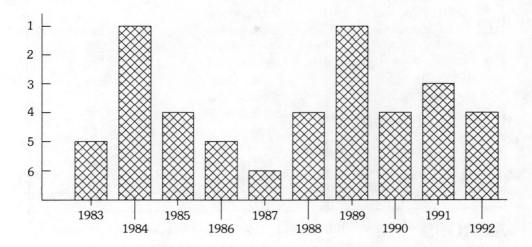

League Leaders 1983-1992

Category	Year	Leader	
Saves	1983	Lee Smith	29
Doubles		Bill Buckner	38 (T)
MVP	1984	Ryne Sandberg	
Cy Young		Rick Sutcliffe	
Winning Pct.		Rick Sutcliffe	.941 (16-1)
Triples		Ryne Sandberg	19 (T)
Runs		Ryne Sandberg	114
MVP	1987	Andre Dawson	
Home Runs		Andre Dawson	49
RBI		Andre Dawson	137
Wins		Rick Sutcliffe	18
Rookie of the Year	1989	Jerome Walton	
Winning Pct.		Mike Bielecki	.720 (18-7)
Runs		Ryne Sandberg	104 (T)
Home Runs	1990	Ryne Sandberg	40
Runs		Ryne Sandberg	116
Cy Young	1992	Greg Maddux	
Wins		Greg Maddux	21 (T)

1992 Leaders

Category	Player	
Batting Average	Mark Grace	.307
Home Runs	Ryne Sandberg	26
RBI	Andre Dawson	90
Stolen Bases	Ryne Sandberg	17
Doubles	Mark Grace	37
Triples	Ryne Sandberg	8
Runs	Ryne Sandberg	100
Hits	Ryne Sandberg	186
Wins	Greg Maddux	20
ERA	Greg Maddux	2.18
Strikeouts	Greg Maddux	199
Saves	Bob Scanlan	14

ACROSS

1. He batted a torrid .647 for the Cubs in the 1989 NLCS, Mark _____ .
5. These were finally installed in Wrigley Field in 1988.
12. Chicago newspaper that owns the Cubs.
13. Rightfielder for the 1984 Eastern Division Champion Cubs, Keith _____ .
14. Shortstop for the 1989 Eastern Division Champion Cubs.
16. Pitching ace for the 1918 National League Champion Cubs, _____ Vaughn.
18. He won 20 games for the Cubs in 1977, Rick _____ .
19. Chicago sportswriter who came up with the idea for a baseball All Star game in 1933, _____ Ward.
22. This Cub reliever won the 1979 Cy Young Award.
23. Realignment would have put the Cubs in the NL _____ .
25. This pitcher posted a 29-9 record for the 1908 World Champion Cubs, Hall of Famer _____ Finger Brown.
28. Left-handed relief specialist Paul .
31. In his best Cub season he went 24-7 for the 1908 World Champs, Ed _____ .

32. Chicago's biggest baseball star of the nineteenth century, Cap _____ .
34. He managed the 1984 Eastern Division Champs.
37. Cub second baseman who died in a 1964 plane crash (two words).
38. The Cubs' 1989 NLCS opponents.
39. This Cub second baseman batted .342 in 1971, _____ Beckert.
41. He played third for the 1989 Cubs for most of the season until they traded for Luis Salazar, Vance _____ .
43. Hall of Fame second baseman on the great Cub teams of 1906-1910, Johnny _____ .
44. Covers the outfield walls at Wrigley Field.
45. This Cub great and Hall of Famer passed away in 1992, Billy _____ .

DOWN

2. He threw the famous "called shot" pitch to Babe Ruth in the 1932 World Series, Charlie _____ .
3. This left-hander went 22-10 for the 1963 Cubs, Dick _____ .
4. Catcher for the 1984 Division Champion Cubs, _____ Davis.

Solution on page 141.

6. He hit the fabled home run into the darkness that sparked the Cubs to the 1938 pennant, Gabby _____ .
7. Third baseman on three Cub pennant winners, in 1935, 1938, and 1945, _____ Hack.
8. Hall of Fame shortstop on the great Cub teams of 1906-1910, Joe _____.
9. Cub manager from 1966 to 1972.
10. Cub shortstop from 1965 to 1975, Don _____ .
11. The Cubs' 1992 pitching ace, Greg _____ .
15. Chicago's team in the ill-fated Federal League of 1914-1915.
17. He posted a 17-9 record for the 1945 National League Champion Cubs, Claude _____ .
20. He played third for the 1984 Division Champion Cubs, Ron _____ .
21. He was traded to the Cubs in June of 1984 and went 16-1 the rest of the way.
24. Cub third baseman from 1960 to '73, Ron _____ .
26. He went 12-6 for the Cubs in 1990, then was slowed by injuries, Mike _____ .
27. Hall of Famer who pitched for Chicago way back in the 1880's, John _____ .
29. Cubs' All Star second baseman, Ryne _____ .
30. Hall of Fame first baseman on the great Cub teams of 1906-1910, Frank ____ .
31. Left fielder on Cub pennant winning teams in 1929 and 1932, _____ Stephenson.
33. Shortstop for the 1984 NL East champs, Larry _____ .
35. Mr. Cub, _____ Banks.
36. He drove in 110 runs for the 1945 NL Champion Cubs, Handy _____ Pafko.
40. Not to be confused with the spaceman of the same name, he was the ace pitcher for Cub pennant winners in 1935 and 1938, Bill _____ .
42. Chicago's TV superstation.

MONTREAL EXPOS

The Expos became the first major league baseball team to establish residence outside of the United States when they joined the National League as part of its 1969 expansion.

They were met with controversy early on, when they tried to trade two of their expansion draft picks, Donn Clendenon and Jesus Alou, to the Houston Astros for Rusty Staub. Clendenon refused to go to Houston, and other players had to be substituted to complete the deal. Staub became the Expos' most popular player, perhaps of all time, and Clendenon stayed with Montreal until mid-season when he was traded to the Mets. In an ironic twist of fate, Clarendon led the Mets to a World Championship and was named World Series MVP.

The Expos started off their first season with a bang. They won their first game, an 11-10 slugfest against the Mets at Shea Stadium and continued the Mets' Opening Day winless streak since they began in 1962. As it turned out, the Mets would win the World Series before they won a season opener.

Nine days later, on April 17, Bill Stoneman took the mound against the Phillies at Connie Mack Stadium and pitched a no-hitter. The Expos went downhill from that point. A lack of pitching and a 20-game losing streak put them out of contention early in the season. The Expos finished 52-110.

Other highlights from the Expos' early years included pitcher Carl Morton's fabulous Rookie of the Year season in 1970 and Stoneman's second no-hitter in 1972.

In 1973, the National League East was embroiled in a tight five-team pennant race. The Expos stayed right in the thick of it until near the end, finishing just three and one-half games out. Manager Gene Mauch relied on the power hitting of Ken Singleton and Bob Bailey, the pinch hitting of Hal Breeden and Boots Day, and the rubber-armed Mike Marshall out of the bullpen to lift the Expos to their best showing to that date.

In the late seventies, the Expos put together a powerful team. The team was led by staff ace Steve Rogers, catcher Gary Carter, third baseman Larry Parrish, and an outfield of Andre Dawson, Warren Cromartie and Ellis Valentine. In 1979, manager Dick Williams led this talented group to a 95-win season and a surprising second place finish, just two games behind the Pittsburgh Pirates.

In 1980, the Expos came close again but got knocked out in the final weekend of the season in a head-on clash with the eventual World Champion Philadelphia Phillies.

The year 1981 marked baseball's infamous strike season. When the players walked off the playing fields on June 11, the Expos trailed the front running Phillies by four games. After the dispute was resolved and play resumed in August, a makeshift split-season scheme was introduced.

The teams in first place in their division when play stopped were crowned the first-half winners. The second half of the season offered the rest of the league a fresh start. The teams with the best records in the second half of the season won the right to meet the first half winners in a best-of-five divisional playoff.

The Expos won the second half, edging out the Cardinals by a half-game, and met the Phillies in the first-ever mini-playoffs. Montreal took the first two games at home, but the Phillies came back to win two in Philadelphia. In the deciding fifth game, Steve Rogers shut out the Phils 3-0 to give the Expos the National League East title.

In the regular playoffs, the Expos ran up against a hot Dodger team. A five-hit shutout by Ray Burris and a clutch three-run homer by Jerry White each accounted for a Montreal victory, but despite this and the torrid hitting of Gary Carter, the Dodgers took the series in five games.

At this point, the Expos were gaining a reputation as perennial pre-season favorites with great teams on paper who couldn't make it to the big dance. After a disappointing fifth place finish in 1984, Buck Rodgers was hired as manager, and the team took on a new look. Gary Carter was dealt to the Mets in a blockbuster trade that brought Hubie Brooks to Montreal.

In 1987, Rodgers led the Expos to a surprising third place finish, winning 91 games and finishing just four games in back of the Cardinals. Tim Wallach led the attack with 123 runs batted in. Hubie Brooks, Tim Raines and Andres Galarraga rounded out a heavy hitting lineup.

In 1992, under new manager Felipe Alou, the Expos enjoyed a most promising season, and they surprised nearly everyone by challenging the Pirates all season for first place. Best of all for Montreal fans, the team is filled with young stars with lots of potential. Young veterans Larry Walker, Delino DeShields, and Marquis Grissom lead an exciting lineup that can only get better as promising young talents Will Cordero, Mel Rojas, Moises Alou, and Sean Berry continue to develop. The Expos have given every indication that they are a team heading in the right direction.

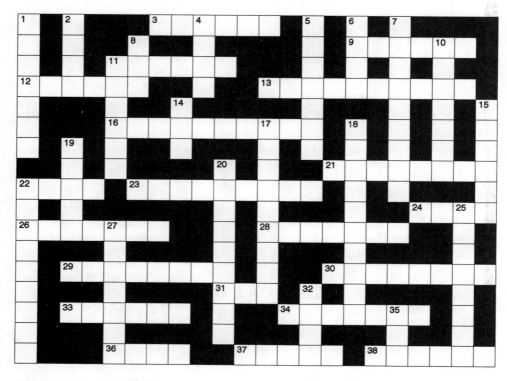

Solution on page 141.

ACROSS

3. This Montreal shortstop drove in 100 runs in 1985, Hubie _____ .

9. Montreal fans called Rusty Staub "Le Grand _____ ".

11. The Expos' 1969 expansion partners.

12. His game-winning homer kept the Expos out of the 1981 World Series, L.A. Dodger Rick _____ .

13. Part time Expo catcher from 1988 to 1991, Nelson _____ .

16. This reliever had a 6-0 record for the Expos in 1988, Andy _____ .

21. This Montreal hurler tossed no-hitters in 1969 and 1972, Bill _____ .

22. He won 18 games for the Expos in 1971 and was named the NL Rookie of the Year, _____ Morton.

23. The Expos' 1992 bullpen ace, John _____ .

24. The Expos' first 20-game winner, _____ Grimsley.

26. Home of the Expos, _____ Stadium.

28. Expo manager from 1985 to 1991, Buck _____ .

29. Utility infielder who batted .353 for the Expos in 1991, Bret _____ .

30. This reliever appeared in 92 games, picking up 31 saves for the Expos in 1973, Mike _____ .

31. This Expo pitcher started and won the 1984 All Star Game, Charlie _____ .

33. This Montreal first baseman was the NL's leading hitter in 1982 with a .331 average, Al _____ .

34. He no-hit the Dodgers for nine innings in 1991 but lost the game in the tenth, Mark _____ .

36. This former Cardinal hurler won 16 games for the Expos in 1992, Ken _____ .

37. He led the Montreal bullpen in 1989 with 9 wins and 28 saves, Tim ____ .
38. This great Expo catcher called it quits in 1992.

DOWN

1. His promising pitching career was hindered by drug problems, hard throwing right-hander Floyd ____ .
2. Third base prospect acquired from the Royals in 1992, ____ Berry.
4. Expos' shortstop from 1989 to 1992, Spike ____ .
5. Expos' manager in 1982, plus parts of 1981 and 1984, Jim ____ .
6. Popular Expo third baseman from 1969, ____ Laboy.
7. Hard-hitting Expo outfielder from the late seventies, Ellis ____ .
8. Pinch hitting specialist for the Expos in the early seventies, Boots ____ .
10. The Expos' leading base stealer in 1991 and 1992, Marquis ____ .
11. He threw a rain-shortened no-hitter against the Cardinals in 1984, David ____ .

14. He was a key pitcher in the Expos' 1981 stretch drive and postseason, ____ Burris.
15. The Expos' leading base stealer throughout the eighties, Tim ____ .
17. Former Expo first baseman known as the Big Cat, Andres ____ .
18. Expo catcher from 1985 to 1991, Mike ____ .
19. The Expos' home from 1969 to 1976, ____ Park.
20. He stole 56 bases for the Expos in 1991, Delino ____ .
22. First baseman for the 1981 NL East Champion Expos, Warren ____ .
25. Middle reliever for Montreal in the middle eighties, Randy ____ (two words).
27. This Expo third baseman hit 30 homers in 1979, Larry ____ .
32. This former Braves outfielder hit 22 homers for the expansion Expos in 1969, ____ Jones.
35. Steve Rogers led the NL in 1982 with a 2.40 ____ .

Division Finishes 1983-1992

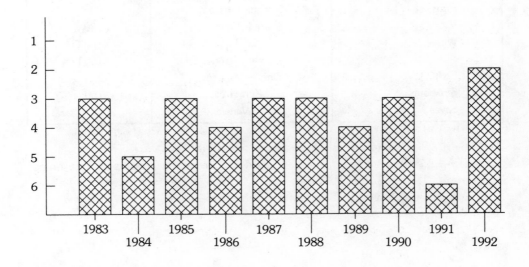

League Leaders 1983-1992

Category	Year	Leader	
Stolen Bases	1983	Tim Raines	90
Doubles		Al Oliver	38 (T)
Runs		Tim Raines	133
Hits		Andre Dawson	189 (T)
RBI	1984	Gary Carter	106 (T)
Stolen Bases		Tim Raines	75
Doubles		Tim Raines	38 (T)
Saves	1985	Jeff Reardon	41
Batting Average	1986	Tim Raines	.334
Triples		Mitch Webster	13
Doubles	1987	Tim Wallach	42
Runs		Tim Raines	133
Doubles	1988	Andres Galarraga	42
Hits		Andres Galarraga	184
Doubles	1989	Tim Wallach	42 (T)
ERA	1991	Dennis Martinez	2.39
Stolen Bases		Marquis Grissom	76
Stolen Bases	1992	Marquis Grissom	78

1992 Leaders

Category	Player	
Batting Average	Larry Walker	.301
Home Runs	Larry Walker	23
RBI	Larry Walker	93
Stolen Bases	Marquis Grissom	78
Doubles	Marquis Grissom	39
Triples	Delino DeShields	8
Runs	Marquis Grissom	99
Hits	Marquis Grissom	180
Wins	Ken Hill	16 (T)
	Dennis Martinez	16 (T)
ERA	Dennis Martinez	2.47
Strikeouts	Ken Hill	150
Saves	John Wetteland	37

NEW YORK METS

From the Sad Sacks of baseball in 1962 to world champions just seven years later, from the infamous Tom Seaver trade in 1977 to Mookie Wilson's grounder through the legs of Bill Buckner in 1986, the history of the New York Mets has been something like a wild roller coaster ride.

In terms of winning championships, the Mets are the most successful expansion baseball team in history. Their two World Series victories rank them equal or better than several teams who have been around since the turn of the century or earlier.

When the Dodgers and Giants left New York for the west coast in 1957, they left behind the broken hearts of millions of New York fans. Every one of their heroes — Willie Mays, Duke Snider, Gil Hodges — was gone, never to return again, or so they thought.

It was in this fertile ground of baseball support that the NL planted the Mets.

The Mets joined the league in 1962 with their expansion partners, the Houston Colt 45's. Unlike the Colts, who were relatively successful in their first season (they finished in eighth place), the Mets were so bad that they won only 40 games and lost 120, a new record for futility. In fact, they lost over 100 games their first four seasons but were still a big hit with the fans.

The cast of characters was legendary. Casey Stengel, now in his seventies and unfazed by the impossible task of making winners out of misfits, provided much of the fun with his colorful personality and "Stengelese" ramblings. Marvelous Marv Throneberry and Choo Choo Coleman became household words, and many older stars like Snider, Hodges and Warren Spahn joined the club to play out their careers.

The Mets' losing ways continued until 1969. The team had been quietly building a pitching staff of young fireballers like Tom Seaver, Jerry Koosman, Nolan Ryan, Gary Gentry and Tug McGraw. When the season began, the Mets had never finished higher than ninth, and any kind of a respectable showing would have been considered a great success.

As the season wore on, the Mets took hold of second place. Then something "amazing" happened. They eclipsed the front-running Cubs, who had led the division all season, then whipped the Braves in the very first NLCS. Then, to everyone's surprise, the Mets beat the overwhelming favorite Baltimore Orioles in the World Series. In only their eighth year of existence, the Mets were World Champions.

Equally amazing, in 1973 the Mets rose from fifth place in early September to win the NL East in a tight five-team race. The Mets then upset the favored Reds in the playoffs and took the A's to seven games in the World Series before falling short.

After '73, the Mets slipped into decline. Superstar Tom Seaver became involved in a salary dispute with management, then found himself the subject of personal attacks by New York sportswriter Dick Young. The surrounding turmoil forced the Mets to trade Seaver to the Reds in 1977. The trade sapped the team of life. They fell back into the cellar and lost many of their fans back to their crosstown rivals, the Yankees, who had returned to their championship ways.

The dark days continued until 1984 when the rebuilding program of new GM Frank Cashen kicked into gear. He added veterans Keith Hernandez and Gary Carter to a line up of young talent that included Darryl Strawberry and Dwight Gooden.

This combination brought the Mets their second World Series title in 1986. In an unforgettably wild postseason, the 1986 team came back from the brink of defeat twice, first in the playoffs, then in the World Series, to take the championship.

In the NLCS, the Mets led 3 games to 2 going into Game 6. When the ninth inning began, they trailed 3-0, and a loss would have forced a seventh game against Astro ace Mike Scott, who was practically unbeatable. New York rallied for three runs in the ninth and forced a nail-biting extra inning affair that the Mets finally won in the 16th.

Then came the World Series. It was Game 6 again, but this time the Mets were down 3 games to 2 and trailing by two runs in the bottom of the tenth with two out and nobody on. One more out would have given the title to the Red Sox and spoiled the Mets' 108-win season.

The Mets refused to die. As the TV camera crews and champagne stood waiting in the Red Sox locker room for the final out, the Mets punched three straight singles to stay alive. A wild pitch scored the tying run, and then came the unforgettable ground ball hit through the legs of first baseman Bill Buckner by Mookie Wilson to score the game winner. Two nights later, a come from behind victory in Game 7 gave the Mets their second title.

Division Finishes 1983-1992

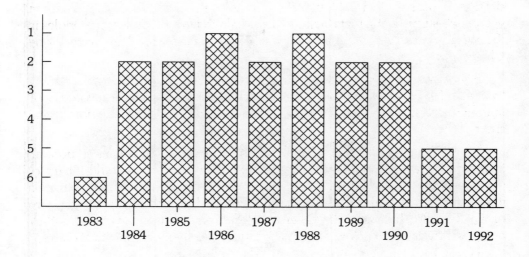

League Leaders 1983-1992

Category	Year	Leader	
Rookie of the Year	1983	Darryl Strawberry	
Rookie of the Year	1984	Doc Gooden	
Strikeouts		Doc Gooden	276
Cy Young	1985	Doc Gooden	
ERA		Doc Gooden	1.53
Wins		Doc Gooden	24
Strikeouts		Doc Gooden	268
Winning Pct.	1986	Bob Ojeda	.783 (18-5)
Winning Pct.	1987	Doc Gooden	.682 (15-7)
Home Runs	1988	Darryl Strawberry	39
Winning Pct.		David Cone	.870 (20-3)
Runs	1989	Howard Johnson	104 (T)
Strikeouts	1990	David Cone	233
Saves		John Franco	33
Doubles		Gregg Jefferies	40
Home Runs	1991	Howard Johnson	38
RBI		Howard Johnson	117
Strikeouts		David Cone	241

1992 Leaders

Category	Player	
Batting Average	Eddie Murray	.261
Home Runs	Eddie Murray	16
RBI	Eddie Murray	93
Stolen Bases	Vince Coleman	24
Doubles	Eddie Murray	37
Triples	Eddie Murray	2 (T)
	Kevin Bass	2 (T)
	Dick Schofield	2 (T)
Runs	Eddie Murray	64
Hits	Eddie Murray	144
Wins	Sid Fernandez	14
ERA	Sid Fernandez	2.73
Strikeouts	David Cone	214
Saves	Anthony Young	15 (T)
	John Franco	15 (T)

ACROSS

1. Sidearm throwing reliever who had a 6-9 record for the Mets in 1992, Jeff _____.

3. He posted an 11-1 record for the 1987 Mets, Terry _____.

6. He played all four infield positions plus the outfield for the 1962 expansion Mets, Hot Rod _____.

8. Former Met Catcher signed by Seattle in 1993, Mackey _____.

10. This former Met was a 1992 Hall of Fame inductee.

11. Howard Johnson.

15. He became Mets manager in 1992.

16. Mets' 1986 NLCS opponent.

18. He stepped in as the Mets closer in 1992 picking up 15 saves, Anthony _____.

20. He played shortstop for the 1962 Mets, _____ Chacon.

22. The starting pitcher for the first ever Mets game in 1962, Roger _____.

23. This rookie right-hander went 13-12 for the '69 Mets and won Game 3 of the World Series, Gary _____.

24. Infielder acquired from the Royals in 1991, Bill _____.

25. Second baseman who came over from Toronto in the David Cone trade, Jeff _____.

26. 1969 World Series MVP, Donn _____.

31. His incredible catch in right field saved Game 4 of the 1969 World Series, Ron _____.

32. Manager of the 1969 championship team (two words).

35. Doctor K.

36. His .340 BA in 1969 is still a Mets season record, _____ Jones.

37. This left-hander posted a 19-12 record with a 2.08 ERA in his rookie year of 1968, Jerry _____.

38. This reliever, known as "The Terminator," began his career with the Mets in 1979.

39. Marvelous Marv.

40. His ERA of 2.43 was best in the NL in 1978, Craig _____.

Solution on page 141.

DOWN

2. Home of the Mets, _____ Stadium.
4. He had a record of 6 wins and 19 losses for the Mets in 1964, Galen _____ .
5. The ace of a pitching-rich staff in 1986 going 18-6 with a 2.57 ERA, Bob _____ .
7. Got the first-ever Mets win in their tenth game in 1962, Jay _____ .
8. He covered left field for the Mets from 1987 to 1991, Kevin _____ .
9. He led the Mets with 14 victories in 1992, Sid _____ .
12. Mets bullpen ace who notched 31 saves in 1984, Jesse _____ .
13. 1986 World Series MVP, Ray _____ .
14. The Mets' 29 million dollar man, Bobby _____ .
17. Two time AL Cy Young Award winner who joined the Mets' pitching staff in 1992, Bret _____ .

19. Mets' 1969 World Series opponents.
21. This reliever was called Jaws for the way he chewed up opposing batters, Skip _____ .
27. His 33 saves topped the National League in 1990, John _____ .
28. Manager of the 1986 World Champion Mets, Dave _____ .
29. He started the first ever Mets game at third base, Don _____ .
30. His 58 stolen bases in 1982 stands as a Met record (first name).
31. He went 12 and 3 for the 1973 NL Champion Mets, George _____ .
33. Standout defensive catcher for the Mets for many years, Jerry _____ .
34. In 1964, this second baseman was the first Met to start an All Star Game, Ron _____ .
35. Catcher for the 1986 World Championship Mets, _____ Carter.

PHILADELPHIA PHILLIES

On October 21, 1980, Tug McGraw threw a fastball past Kansas City outfielder Willie Wilson for a called strike three. The Veterans Stadium crowd erupted to celebrate an event for which they had waited 97 years. The Philadelphia Phillies were finally baseball's World Champions.

The beginnings of the '80 championship team can be traced back to a 1972 trade in which the Phillies traded Rick Wise to acquire pitcher Steve Carlton from the Cardinals. Carlton made his presence felt immediately, winning 27 games and the Cy Young Award for a last place Phillie club in 1972. What made this feat even more remarkable was that the Phillies only won 59 games that year, which meant the big lefty was responsible for nearly half of them.

The Phillies' rise to the baseball forefront coincided with the emergence of the player considered by many to be the greatest Phillie of all time, Mike Schmidt. Schmidt erased memories of a difficult rookie season in which he batted only .196 by winning three straight NL home run titles (1974-1976). Paired with "The Bull," Greg Luzinski, Schmidt led the most feared one-two slugging attack in baseball.

The Phillies won division titles three years in a row in 1976-78 but failed to best the NL West Champs in the playoffs. In 1976, they were swept by the eventual World Champion Cincinnati Reds in three games. The next two years, they suffered disappointing losses to the Dodgers, losing in four games both times.

Frustration was peaking in Philadelphia, among both the team and the fans. It wasn't enough to be one of baseball's best teams. Nothing short of a World Series title would do. After all, the Phillies were baseball's only non-expansion team never to have won a world championship.

Frustration was nothing new for the Phillies. It started with their first season back in 1883. In those early days, they were contenders more often than not. Their teams contained an array of future Hall of Famers. In 1894, Sam Thompson batted .404, Ed Delahanty .400, and Billy Hamilton .399 as the Phillies came within a whisker of having baseball's only .400 outfield. Hamilton scored 196 runs that year, which is still a major league record.

They also had a few other players destined for Cooperstown, second baseman Napoleon Lajoie and outfielder Elmer Flick. As the twentieth century began, the Phillies appeared to be poised for greatness. However, the player raids by the

86

upstart American League hit the Phillies hard. Worse yet for the Phillies, the AL placed their own team in Philadelphia, the A's, whose record for greatness the Phillies would never be able to match.

The Phillies won their first NL pennant in 1915, behind the pitching of the immortal Grover Cleveland Alexander. Pete, as he was called, won 31 games that year, 12 of them shutouts, and led the league with an ERA of 1.22. Outfielder Gavvy Cravath led the league with 24 home runs, a remarkable total for the dead-ball era. The Phils met the Boston Red Sox in the World Series and lost, four games to one.

It wasn't until 1950 that the Phils returned to the spotlight. On the last day of the season, Dick Sisler hit a tenth-inning three run homer against the Brooklyn Dodgers that put the Phillies into the World Series for the first time in 35 years.

The '50 team, known as the "Whiz Kids," was led by Richie Ashburn, Del Ennis, and pitchers Robin Roberts and Curt Simmons, all in their early twenties. They also had the league's MVP that year, relief pitcher Jim Konstanty, who posted 16 wins and 22 saves. Unfortunately, the Whiz Kids ran out of magic in the World Series. They were swept in four straight by the mighty New York Yankees.

After contending for a few years after 1950, the Phillies fell on hard times. They hit rock bottom in 1961 posting a dismal 47-107 record. Fortunately for the Phils, this poor showing was eclipsed the following year by the expansion New York Mets, who finished at 40-120 and set a new modern record for futility.

The Phillies of 1964 looked as though they were going to win the NL title as they held a six and a half game lead with only twelve games left to play. However, they proceeded to lose ten games in a row to lose the pennant by one game in one of baseball's most famous collapses.

After 1978's playoff loss, the Phillies could have accepted their 95 years of futility. Instead, they took the steps needed to add the pieces to the winning puzzle. In 1979, they signed free agent Pete Rose, and midway through the season, Dallas Green was brought in to replace Danny Ozark as manager. Rose and Green brought a winning attitude to Philadelphia, the perfect complement to the Phillies' already talented team make-up. Putting it all together in 1980 enabled the Phillies to finally shed the image of "also-rans."

The Phillies made one last run at the crown in 1983. The "Wheeze Kids," as they were jokingly called, included aged stars Rose, Joe Morgan, and Tony Perez. Cy Young Award winner John Denny led the Phillies past their old nemesis,the Dodgers, in the playoffs into the World Series against the Baltimore Orioles. There the Wheeze Kids sputtered, losing in five games.

Phillie fans are already preparing for the induction of Mike Schmidt and Steve Carlton into the Hall of Fame upon their eligibility in 1994 and 1995, respectively. Schmidt's three MVP awards and Carlton's four Cy Young Awards have earned them their place among baseball's all-time greats.

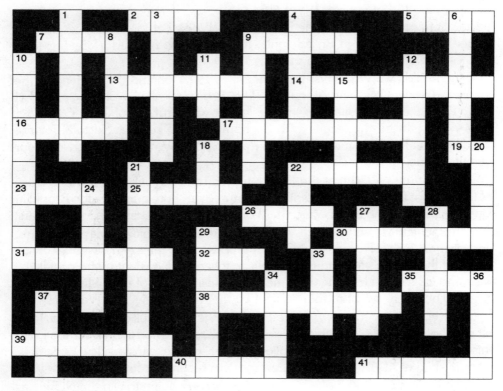

Solution on page 142.

ACROSS

2. This Phillie led the National League in hitting for much of 1992, John _____ .

5. Shortstop for the 1980 World Champion Phillies, Larry _____ .

7. What they called Greg Luzinski.

9. He managed the Phillies to three division titles in 1976-1978, Danny _____ .

13. He replaced Nick Leyva as Phillies manager in April of 1991, Jim _____ .

14. Hall of Fame slugger for the Phillies in the 1890's, Big Ed _____ .

16. Led the 1983 NL Champion Phillies with a 19-6 record, John _____ .

17. He won 31 games for the 1915 National League champion Phillies, Grover Cleveland _____ .

19. Shortstop (abbrev.).

22. Phillies' opponent in the 1980 World Series.

23. What Mitch Williams throws.

25. Clutch performer in the 1980 World Series, outfielder Del _____ .

26. Phils' second baseman in the mid-seventies, Dave _____ .

30. He retired in 1989 with 548 career homers.

31. This Phillie catcher had his best season ever in 1992, Darren _____ .

32. Phillies' slugger from the 1890's, Hall of Famer _____ Thompson.

35. Managed the Phillies in 1987 and 1988, Lee _____ .

38. Phillies' bullpen ace who notched 40 saves in 1987, Steve _____ .

39. Relief ace for the 1983 NL Champion Phils, Al _____ .

40. Rightfielder for the 1950 Whiz Kids, Del _____ .

41. Second baseman for the 1980 World Champs, Manny _____ .

DOWN

1. He pitched a perfect game against the Mets on Fathers' Day in 1964.
3. He won 20 games for the 1950 Whiz Kids, Robin _____ .
4. The Secretary of Defense, Garry ____ .
6. Played first base for the 1950 Whiz Kids, Eddie _____ .
8. Steve Carlton.
9. Phillies' 1983 World Series opponent.
10. Willie Jones, also known as _____ , was the Phillies' Whiz Kid third baseman in 1950.
11. The Phillies got him from the Indians in exchange for Julio Franco and four others in 1982, _____ Hayes.
12. All Star catcher for the Phillies in 1988, Lance _____ .
15. He hit .325 for the Phillies in 1990, _____ Dykstra.
18. Phillies GM, _____ Thomas.

20. This left-hander won 20 games for the 1966 Phillies, Chris _____ .
21. He no-hit the Giants on August 15, 1990.
22. First baseman for the 1980 World Champion Phils.
24. Phillies' second baseman throughout the sixties, Tony _____ .
27. He picked up a win and four saves in the 1980 postseason for the Phils.
28. His home run won the pennant for the 1950 Phils, Dick _____ .
29. Phillies' All Star centerfielder of the 1950's, Richie _____ .
33. This Phillies pitcher tossed a no-hitter against Cincinnati in 1971, Rick ____ .
34. Spent most of the eighties as a pinch hitter for the Phils, Greg _____ .
36. Phillies' outfielder whose father played shortstop for the Phils in the sixties.
37. Phillies' shortstop from 1989 to 1991, Dickie _____ .

Division Finishes 1983-1992

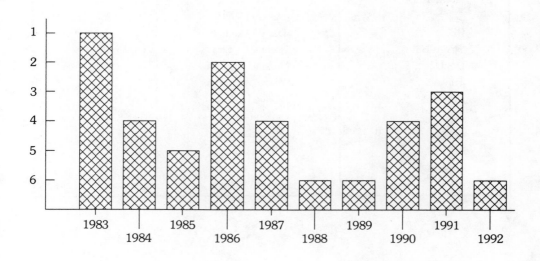

League Leaders 1983-1992

Category	Year	Leader	
Cy Young	1983	John Denny	
Home Runs		Mike Schmidt	40
Wins		John Denny	19
Winning Pct.		John Denny	.760 (19-6)
Strikeouts		Steve Carlton	275
Home Runs	1984	Mike Schmidt	36 (T)
RBI		Mike Schmidt	106 (T)
Triples		Juan Samuel	19 (T)
MVP	1986	Mike Schmidt	
Home Runs		Mike Schmidt	37
RBI		Mike Schmidt	119
Doubles		Von Hayes	46
Runs		Von Hayes	107 (T)
Cy Young	1987	Steve Bedrosian	
Saves		Steve Bedrosian	40
Triples		Juan Samuel	15
Hits	1990	Lenny Dykstra	192 (T)
RBI	1992	Darren Daulton	109

1992 Leaders

Category	Player	
Batting Average	John Kruk	.323
Home Runs	Dave Hollins	27 (T)
	Darren Daulton	27 (T)
RBI	Darren Daulton	109
Stolen Bases	Lenny Dykstra	30
Doubles	Mariano Duncan	40
Triples	Mickey Morandini	8
Runs	Dave Hollins	104
Hits	John Kruk	164
Wins	Curt Schilling	14
ERA	Curt Schilling	2.35
Strikeouts	Curt Schilling	147
Saves	Mitch Williams	29

PITTSBURGH PIRATES

The Pittsburgh Pirates dominated baseball at the turn of the century, capturing National League pennants in 1901, 1902 and 1903. Their on-field exploits paced the league at a time when the infamous baseball wars between the established National League and the upstart American League commanded off-the-field attention.

The existence of the new league offered NL players an alternative to the low salaries paid by the NL and many stars jumped. The Pirates were the only NL team to emerge relatively untouched by the raids, and their record showed it.

Hall of Famer Fred Clarke, a fierce competitor and prolific baserunner, was the Pirates player-manager, but the biggest star was shortstop Honus Wagner. One of the best hitters of his day, the Flying Dutchman is still generally regarded as the best shortstop to ever play the game.

In 1903, the two leagues were finally at peace, and the first World Series was played between the Pirates and the American League Champion, the Boston Pilgrims. Wagner slumped in the Series, and Boston hurlers Bill Dineen and Cy Young steered the Pilgrims to the championship.

The Pirates won the pennant again in 1909, winning 110 games along the way, and defeated the Detroit Tigers for their first World Series victory. This Series was noteworthy because it brought together, for the first time, baseball's two best players, Wagner and Detroit's Ty Cobb. Just as Wagner had a bad Series in 1903, Cobb struggled in the 1909 Series, and the Pirates prevailed in seven games.

In the mid-1920's, the Pirates enjoyed a resurgence, winning pennants in 1925 and 1927. The 1925 squad featured future Hall of Famers third baseman Pie Traynor, and outfielders Kiki Cuyler and Max Carey. Their 1925 World Series opponents were the defending champions, the Washington Senators. The closely contested Series went seven games. Early in Game 7, the Pirates trailed by four runs, but they eventually overcame the pitching mastery of the great Walter Johnson to take the game, 9-7, and the Series.

In 1927, Lloyd Waner joined his brother Paul on the Bucs, and they took the pennant again. This time they had the misfortune of running into the New York Yankees and "Murderer's Row" in the World Series. The team widely regarded

91

as the greatest of all time swept the Pirates in four games. It may not have made a difference, but Pittsburgh fans couldn't figure out why Pirate manager Donie Bush would not allow Kiki Cuyler to play at all in the World Series. This remains to this day one of baseball's great mysteries.

The Pirates fielded generally poor teams for the next 30 years. Slugger Ralph Kiner led or tied for the NL lead in home runs his first seven seasons, 1946-1952, but his heroics alone weren't usually enough to keep the Pirates out of last place. Not until 1960 did the Pirates make it back to the Series. The opposition was once again the New York Yankees, this time with Mantle and Maris replacing Ruth and Gehrig.

After six games, the Series was deadlocked at 3-3. The Pirates won their three games by scores of 6-4, 3-2, and 5-2, while the Yankees blew the Bucs out of the park in their three wins, 16-3, 10-0, and 12-0. Game 7 was a roller coaster affair with several lead changes. The game was finally decided by Bill Mazeroski's memorable ninth inning homer. The Pirates won the Series, exacting revenge for their 1927 defeat.

During the sixties, the Pirates powerful offense featured hitting stars Roberto Clemente, Willie Stargell, Matty Alou, Al Oliver and Manny Sanguillen, but the Bucs always seemed to lack pitching. It was in the early seventies that the Pirates finally put it all together. Between 1970 and 1975, the Pirates dominated the NL East, winning five division titles. In 1971, Roberto Clemente led the Pirates over the Orioles in the World Series in what turned out to be his last game.

On New Year's Day, 1972, the Pirates and all of baseball suffered a huge loss as Clemente died in a plane crash while bringing supplies to earthquake victims in Central America. Under special circumstances, the five year wait was waived and Clemente was elected to the Hall of Fame in 1973.

The reins of team leadership passed to Willie Stargell. At the age of 39, Stargell enjoyed an MVP season as he led the Bucs to the 1979 World Championship. The Pirates again met the Baltimore Orioles in the World Series and trailed three games to one but fought off elimination and won the seventh game on Stargell's clutch home run. Stargell and slugger Dave Parker led the Pittsburgh "family" to its second championship of the seventies.

When Jim Leyland took over as Pirate manager in 1986, he inherited a last place team. Patiently, he built the Pirates into a powerhouse. Sluggers Barry Bonds and Bobby Bonilla, second baseman Jose Lind, and pitching stars Doug Drabek and John Smiley formed the nucleus of the Pirate teams that won NL East titles from 1990 to 1992. Each year, though, the Bucs suffered disappointing losses in the playoffs.

The most heartbreaking of the three setbacks came in 1992, when the Atlanta Braves pulled off an amazing ninth inning rally in Game 7 to spoil a gutsy pitching performance by Pirate ace Doug Drabek.

Division Finishes 1983-1992

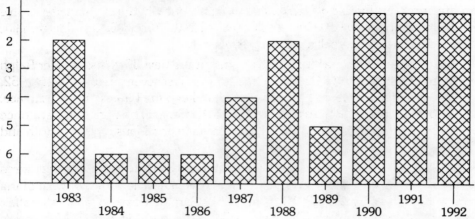

League Leaders 1983-1992

Category	Year	Leader	
Batting Average	1983	Bill Madlock	.323
Doubles		Johnny Ray	38 (T)
Doubles	1984	Johnny Ray	38 (T)
Triples	1988	Andy Van Slyke	15
MVP	1990	Barry Bonds	
Cy Young		Doug Drabek	
Wins		Doug Drabek	22
Winning Pct.		Doug Drabek	.786 (22-6)
Wins	1991	John Smiley	20 (T)
Winning Pct.		John Smiley	.714 (20-8) (T)
Doubles		Bobby Bonilla	44
MVP	1992	Barry Bonds	
Doubles		Andy Van Slyke	45
Runs		Barry Bonds	109
Hits		Andy Van Slyke	199 (T)

1992 Leaders

Category	Player	
Batting Average	Andy Van Slyke	.324
Home Runs	Barry Bonds	34
RBI	Barry Bonds	103
Stolen Bases	Barry Bonds	39
Doubles	Andy Van Slyke	45
Triples	Andy Van Slyke	12
Runs	Barry Bonds	109
Hits	Andy Van Slyke	199
Wins	Doug Drabek	15
ERA	Doug Drabek	2.77
Strikeouts	Doug Drabek	177
Saves	Stan Belinda	18

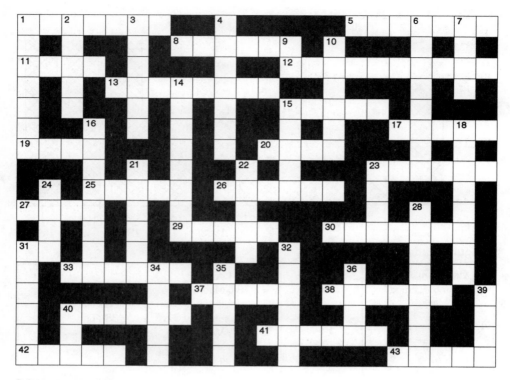

Solution on page 142.

ACROSS

1. He was the catcher for the 1960 World Champion Pirates, Smokey _____ .

5. Pirate infielder from the 70's whose name is now synonymous with a below .200 batting average.

8. This Pirate slugger was the 1978 NL MVP.

11. Second baseman for the 1990-1992 NL East Champion Bucs, Jose _____ .

12. Pirate manager since 1986 (two words).

13. This Pirate outfielder fell one hit shy of 200 in 1992.

15. Pirate Gold Glove shortstop from the 1960's, Gene _____ .

17. This Buc hurler no-hit the Mets in September of 1969, Bob _____ .

19. He played centerfield for the Bucs in 1966 and batted .342, Matty _____ .

20. This outfielder batted .321 for the Bucs in 1984, Lee _____ .

23. Legendary Pirate shortstop, Honus _____ .

25. _____ Rivers Stadium.

26. Great Pirate reliever from the early seventies, Dave _____ .

27. He played outfield for the Bucs in 1966 and batted .332, Manny _____ .

29. Pirate pinch hitter from the sixties, Jerry _____ .

30. He saved 31 games for the World Champion Pirates in 1979, Kent _____ .

31. Complete game (abbrev.).

33. This Pirate hurler led the team in wins in 1986 with 15, Rick _____ .

37. Hall of Fame Pittsburgh outfielder from 1911 to 1926, Max _____ .

38. Pirate broadcaster and former pitcher who once had to walk home after the Bucs blew a big lead, Jim _____ .

40. This left-hander represented the Pirates on the 1990 All Star team, Neal ____ .

41. He pitched perfect ball against the Braves for 12 innings in 1959, but lost the game, Harvey ____ .

42. His Number 4 hangs on the outfield wall, Hall of Famer ____ Kiner.

43. This Buc fireballer led the NL in strikeouts in 1964 with 250, Bob ____ .

DOWN

1. He led the Bucs with 18 saves in 1992, Stan ____ .

2. This left-hander had a 14-9 record for the Bucs in 1992, ____ Tomlin.

3. They called him "Dr. Strangeglove," Dick ____ .

4. Hall of Fame third baseman for the Bucs, some call him the best ever, Pie ____ .

6. In 1956 this Buc first baseman hit 8 home runs in 8 consecutive games (two words).

7. This lefty joined the Bucs in the 1990 stretch drive and went 6-2, ____ Smith.

9. Pirate outfielder from 1985 to 1990, ____ Reynolds.

10. He won 20 games for the Bucs in 1991, John ____ .

14. Pittsburgh's Number 8, Hall of Famer Willie ____ .

15. He won three games for the Pirates against the Tigers in the 1909 World Series, Babe ____ .

16. Manager of the 1960 and 1971 World Champion Pirates, Danny ____ .

18. Second baseman for the 1979 World Champion Pirates, Rennie ____ .

21. He won 18 games for the Bucs in 1960 but lost 2 to the Yanks in the World Series, Bob ____ .

22. This DiMaggio brother played for the Pirates.

23. He pitched a beauty to keep the Bucs alive in Game 5 of the 1992 NLCS, Bob ____ .

24. His best year for the Bucs was 1990 when he won 22 games, ____ Drabek.

28. This Pirate great was the National League MVP in 1966.

31. Pirate Hall of Famer from the 1920's, Kiki ____ .

32. He went 12 and 9 as a Pirate rookie in 1966, Woody ____ .

34. Catcher for the 1979 World Champion Pirates (two words).

35. Pirate Hall of Famers Paul and Lloyd.

36. Shortstop for the 1979 World Champion Pirates, Tim ____ .

39. This Pirate reliever posted an incredible 18-1 record in 1959, Roy ____ .

40. This Pirate catcher blasted a three run homer in the eighth inning of Game 7 of the 1960 World Series, ____ Smith.

ST. LOUIS CARDINALS

The St. Louis Cardinals are the most successful team in the history of the National League. In addition to winning nine World Series championships, they have also been one of baseball's most colorful teams with a tremendous history of legendary players and heroic performances.

The Cardinals entered the National League in 1892 but did not win their first pennant until 1926. Before then, the ballclub floundered in the NL's second division although three of their managers during this period made it to the Hall of Fame: Roger Bresnahan, Miller Huggins, and Branch Rickey.

In 1915, a young infielder named Rogers Hornsby was called up from the minors and began to develop into one of the greatest hitters in the game. In 1925, Hornsby took over the team as player-manager, and, the next year, the Cards won their first pennant and the right to face the American League champion New York Yankees in the World Series. The 1926 fall classic provided the stage for the first of the great Cardinal legends.

In the seventh game, the Cardinals took a 3-2 lead into the seventh inning. The Yankees loaded the bases with two out. Tony Lazzeri was stepping up to the plate, and St. Louis pitcher, Jesse Haines, had developed a blister on his pitching hand. Hornsby stopped the game and called for Grover Cleveland Alexander to come in.

Alexander had once been baseball's greatest pitcher. Since that time, he had developed a well-known drinking problem and a not-so-well-known battle with epilepsy. He came to the Cards in mid-season and had contributed to the pennant-winning effort. He already had two victories in the World Series and, legend has it, was sleeping off a late-night binge in the bullpen when Hornsby sent out the call.

Nevertheless, he ambled in to face Lazzeri. On Alexander's second pitch, Lazzeri connected and sent a screamer down the left field line that just barely went foul. The Yankee Stadium crowd went wild, but Alexander stayed calm and held on to strike him out. The threat over, the Cards held on to win their first World Championship.

The next Cardinal championship came in 1931. This time the opponents were Connie Mack's Philadelphia Athletics, who were looking to pick up their third straight World Series title. The A's were stopped almost single-handedly by the Cardinals' centerfielder, Pepper Martin. Martin delivered clutch hitting, made great fielding plays, and ran wild on the bases to the dismay of A's catcher Mickey Cochrane.

Martin batted .500 in the Series with four doubles, one homer, five RBI, and five stolen bases. The Cards won in seven games, spoiling Mack's last World Series appearance.

In 1934, Frankie Frisch was the player-manager of a spirited NL pennant champion Cardinal team known as "the Gas House Gang." This crew included Martin, Ducky Medwick, Ripper Collins, Leo Durocher, and the pitching duo of Dizzy and Daffy Dean.

The Gas House gang beat the Detroit Tigers in the World Series in seven games. The series is most memorable because of the near riot in the seventh game after Ducky Medwick slid hard into Tiger third baseman, Marv Owen. During the next inning, Tiger fans pelted Medwick with garbage, forcing play to stop. Commissioner Landis, who was attending the game, ordered Medwick removed from the game for his own safety. It didn't affect the outcome as the Cardinals won the game eleven to nothing..

In 1942, a young Cardinal team took the National League pennant by winning 106 games. The pitching aces that year were Mort Cooper and Johnny Beazley, and the offense was led by Enos Slaughter and a 21-year-old outfielder named Stan Musial. The Cards took the Series in five games from a star studded Yankees team.

In 1946, MVP Stan Musial led the Cards to a regular season tie with the Brooklyn Dodgers, the first time this had happened in baseball history. A best two-of-three playoff was set up, and St. Louis swept the Dodgers to take the pennant.

The 1946 World Series against the Red Sox will always be remembered for Enos Slaughter's "mad dash to home," as he caught everyone by surprise by scoring from first on a base hit with the winning run in the seventh and final game.

The Cardinals have won three more championships in the post-Musial years. Ken Boyer capped an MVP season by leading his Cards to a seven game victory over the Yankees in the 1964 Series. That year the Cards acquired outfielder Lou Brock in a trade with the Cubs.

In 1967, Bob Gibson was nearly unhittable in the Series, contributing three complete game wins while leading the Cards over the Red Sox. The next season, Gibson won the Cy Young after posting a 22-9 record and an unbelievable 1.12 ERA. The Cardinals returned to the Series but lost to Detroit.

The Cardinals won another championship in 1982. Manager Whitey Herzog's squad, led by Keith Hernandez and Ozzie Smith, took the Milwaukee Brewers in seven games.

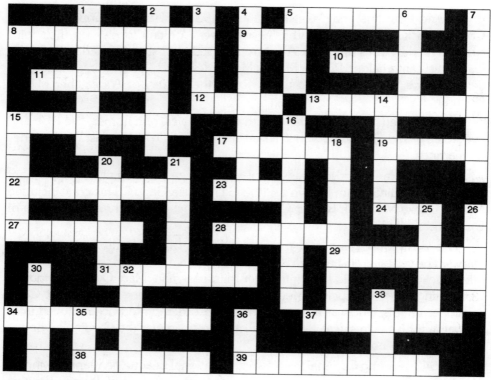

Solution on page 142.

ACROSS

5. Cardinals' Hall of Fame second baseman, Rogers _____ .

8. Famous baseball broadcaster who started out as a Cardinal catcher in the 1940's, Joe _____ .

9. Cardinals' bullpen ace since 1990, _____ Smith.

10. The Gas _____ Gang.

11. Second baseman on the St. Louis pennant winning clubs of the sixties, Julian _____ .

12. He managed the Cards' opponents in the 1964 World Series. (first name)

13. He got three wins for the Cards in the 1946 World Series against Boston, Harry "The Cat" _____ .

15. This team's collapse in 1964 allowed the Cards to win the pennant.

17. Manager of the 1931 World Champion Cardinals, Gabby _____ .

19. The Cardinals' wizard at shortstop, _____ Smith.

22. Cardinals' All Star catcher in 1992, Tom _____ .

23. This former Expo won 12 games for the Cards in 1991, _____ Smith.

24. Long time Cardinal manager, _____ Schoendienst.

27. This actor played the part of Grover Cleveland Alexander in the movie, *The Winning Team*.

28. This Hall of Famer pitched for the Cardinals from 1920 to 1937, Jesse _____ .

29. This Cardinal hurler won 21 games in 1960, Ernie _____ .

31. Third baseman for the 1967 World Champion Cardinals, Mike _____ .

34. Hall of Fame first baseman for the 1926 and 1931 Cardinal champion clubs, Sunny Jim _____ .
37. The last time a Cardinal pitcher won this award was in 1970 (two words).
38. "Stan the Man."
39. He won 30 games for the Cards in 1934, the last National League pitcher to do it (two words).

DOWN

1. Shortstop for the 1967 World Champion Cards, Dal _____ .
2. Bullpen ace for the Cards' pennant winning teams in 1967 and 1968, Joe _____ .
3. This Cardinal Hall of Famer led the NL in hitting in 1931 with a .349 average, Chick _____ .
4. Cardinals' rightfielder on their 1942 and 1946 championship teams, Enos _____ .
5. This Cardinal second baseman knocked in 110 runs in 1985, Tommy _____ .
6. _____ Memorial Stadium, home of the Cardinals.
7. Cardinal relief ace from the early sixties, Lindy _____ .

14. St. Louis brother-battery in the 1940's, Mort and Walker _____ .
15. This rookie led the Cardinals to an upset victory in the 1931 World Series against the A's, _____ Martin.
16. This Cardinal first baseman was the National League's MVP in 1979, Keith _____ .
18. This right-hander posted a 16-5 record for the Cards in 1992, Bob _____ .
20. Cards' 1985 World Series opponent.
21. His microscopic 1.12 ERA in 1968 led all major league pitchers, Bob _____ .
25. This hard luck right-hander had a 7-19 record for the Cards in 1990, Jose _____ .
26. He played centerfield for the Cards in the 1960's, Curt _____ .
30. This Cardinal Hall of Famer retired in 1979 with 938 career stolen bases.
32. Cardinal manager from 1959 to 1961, Solly _____ .
33. This Cardinal outfielder batted .305 in 1991, Felix _____ .
35. Catcher for Cardinal championship teams in 1964 and 1967, _____ McCarver.
36. Al Hrabosky was known as the _____ Hungarian.

Division Finishes 1983-1992

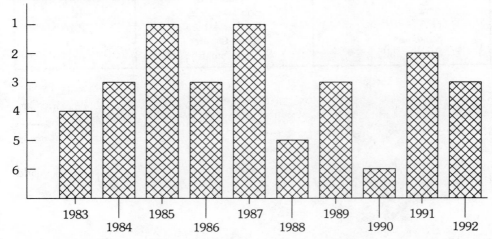

League Leaders 1983-1992

Category	Year	Leader	
Wins	1984	Joaquin Andujar	20
Saves		Bruce Sutter	45
MVP	1985	Willie McGee	
Rookie of the Year		Vince Coleman	
Batting Average		Willie McGee	.353
Stolen Bases		Vince Coleman	110
Triples		Willie McGee	18
Hits		Willie McGee	216
Rookie of the Year	1986	Todd Worrell	
Stolen Bases		Vince Coleman	107
Saves		Todd Worrell	36
Stolen Bases	1987	Vince Coleman	109
ERA	1988	Joe Magrane	2.18
Stolen Bases		Vince Coleman	81
Strikeouts	1989	Jose DeLeon	201
Stolen Bases		Vince Coleman	65
Doubles		Pedro Guerrero	42 (T)
Batting Average	1990	Willie McGee	.335
Stolen Bases		Vince Coleman	77
Saves	1991	Lee Smith	47
Triples		Ray Lankford	15
Winning Pct.	1992	Bob Tewksbury	.762 (16-5)
Saves		Lee Smith	43

1992 Leaders

Category	Player	
Batting Average	Felix Jose	.295
Home Runs	Ray Lankford	20
RBI	Ray Lankford	86
Stolen Bases	Ozzie Smith	43
Doubles	Ray Lankford	40
Triples	Luis Alicea	12
Runs	Ray Lankford	87
Hits	Ray Lankford	175
Wins	Bob Tewksbury	16
ERA	Bob Tewksbury	2.16
Strikeouts	Omar Olivares	124
Saves	Lee Smith	43

ATLANTA BRAVES

Baseball's oldest franchise, the Atlanta Braves, began playing in 1871. They were known initially as the Boston Red Stockings and changed their name to the Beaneaters during the 1890's. Not until after the turn of the century did the team become the Boston Braves.

Early Braves' history is highlighted by the 1914 "Miracle Braves," a team that shocked the baseball world by shooting from last place in mid-July to the pennant. The miracle continued in the World Series; the Braves walloped the heavily-favored Philadelphia Athletics in the first four game sweep in World Series history.

It wasn't until 1948 that the Braves returned to the World Series. Led by the pitching duo of Johnny Sain and Warren Spahn, league MVP Bob Elliott, and sparkplug infielders Eddie Stanky and Al Dark, the Braves faced off against the AL champion, the Cleveland Indians. The Braves lost in six games.

The Braves could never displace the Red Sox as first in the hearts of Boston fans. Severely declining attendance in the early fifties forced a franchise move to Milwaukee, the first such move in modern-day baseball.

The fans of Milwaukee immediately embraced the Braves. Attendance zoomed to over a million their first year in the city. Hall of Fame sluggers Hank Aaron and Eddie Mathews and pitchers Spahn and Lew Burdette led the Braves back to baseball prominence. The Braves defeated the Yankees in 1957 to capture the franchise's second world championship. The teams met up again in the fall classic of '58, but the Yankees came out on top that time.

The team started to falter in the sixties, and poor attendance followed. As a result, the owners picked up the franchise and moved to Atlanta in 1966, enraging Milwaukee fans and making the Braves the first team ever to move twice.

Throughout the ups and downs experienced by the Braves, Hank Aaron remained a constant force. In 1969, with the advent of divisional play, Aaron led the Braves to the first NL West title.

The nation focused its attention upon Aaron and the Braves as the 1974 season began. Aaron was poised to break Babe Ruth's all-time career home run record of 714. On April 8th, Aaron did just that, hammering an Al Downing pitch out of Fulton County Stadium. Aaron returned to Milwaukee in 1975 and finished his career as baseball's most prolific home run hitter in '76, with a total of 755.

A different slugger, Dale Murphy led the Braves to their second NL West title in 1982. New skipper Joe Torre piloted the Braves to a 13-0 start and kept them in first through the end of the season. Disappointingly, the Cardinals swept the Braves in the playoffs 3-0.

Murphy provided most of the Braves' high points during the 1980's, winning back-to-back MVP awards in 1982 and 1983 while posting some big numbers. Braves fans had little else to cheer about, though, as the Braves hovered at or near last place throughout the decade.

So far, the nineties have proven much more successful for the Braves. In 1991, after finishing last for three straight seasons, the Braves came out on top of a tight pennant race by overtaking the Dodgers and winning the NL West.

The Braves rode the young arms of John Smoltz, Steve Avery , and Cy Young Award winner Tom Glavine, the powerful bats of league MVP Terry Pendleton, 30-30 man Ron Gant, and Dave Justice into the playoffs against the Pittsburgh Pirates. It took seven games, but the Braves managed to put the Pirates down for their first NLCS success.

The Minnesota Twins provided the opposition in the first World Series to feature two teams that had finished last in their divisions the previous season, making 1991 the first "last-to-first" World Series.

The match-up proved to be one of the most exciting World Series ever. The Braves dropped Games 1 and 2 in the noisy Metrodome. Back in Atlanta, the Braves took Game 3 on a twelfth inning RBI single by Mark Lemke and Game 4 on a ninth inning sacrifice fly by journeyman catcher Jerry Willard. A 14-5 blowout win in Game 5 sent the Braves back to Minnesota needing just one win for the World Championship. The win never came. Kirby Puckett won Game 6 with a dramatic eleventh inning homer, and Atlanta came up 1-0 losers in a game that featured an incredible pitching duel between John Smoltz and the Twins winning pitcher Jack Morris.

In 1992 the Braves won again in the NL West, eight games ahead of second place Cincinnati. Although they had an easier time winning the division title than the year before, they faced an even more determined Pittsburgh team in the NLCS.

The Pirates, after falling behind three games to one, beat the Braves in Games 5 and 6 to force a seventh game finale. The Pirates held a 2-0 lead going into the bottom of the ninth, and the end of a great Braves season was only three outs away. The Braves staged an amazing comeback highlighted by Francisco Cabrera's pinch single to left as Justice scored from third with the tying run, followed by Bream who barely slid past the tag of Pirates catcher Mike LaValliere with the winning run.

This furious finish got the Braves into the World Series against the AL Champion Toronto Blue Jays, who took the Series in six games. The Jays victory prevented the Braves from becoming the first team ever to win a world championship in three different cities.

Division Finishes 1983-1992

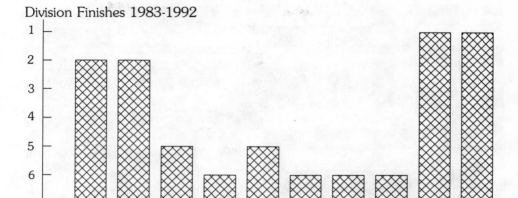

League Leaders 1983-1992

Category	Year	Leader	
MVP	1983	Dale Murphy	
RBI		Dale Murphy	121
Triples		Brett Butler	13
Home Runs	1984	Dale Murphy	36 (T)
Home Runs	1985	Dale Murphy	37
Runs		Dale Murphy	118
Rookie of the Year	1990	David Justice	
MVP	1991	Terry Pendleton	
Cy Young		Tom Glavine	
Batting Average		Terry Pendleton	.319
Wins		Tom Glavine	20 (T)
Hits		Terry Pendleton	187
Wins	1992	Tom Glavine	21 (T)
Strikeouts		John Smoltz	215
Triples		Deion Sanders	14
Hits		Terry Pendleton	199 (T)

1992 Leaders

Category	Player	
Batting Average	Terry Pendleton	.311
Home Runs	David Justice	21 (T)
	Terry Pendleton	21 (T)
RBI	Terry Pendleton	105
Stolen Bases	Otis Nixon	41
Doubles	Terry Pendleton	39
Triples	Deion Sanders	14
Runs	Terry Pendleton	98
Hits	Terry Pendleton	199
Wins	Tom Glavine	20
ERA	Tom Glavine	2.76
Strikeouts	John Smoltz	215
Saves	Alejandro Pena	15

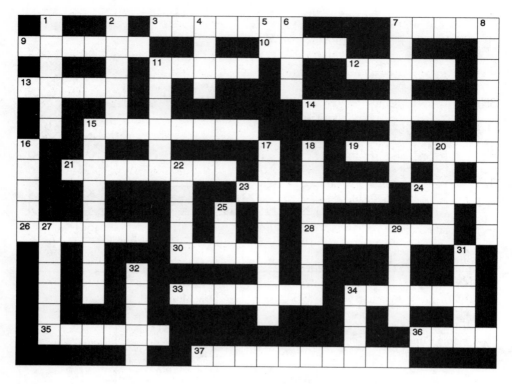

Solution on page 143.

ACROSS

3. He blasted 28 homers in his rookie
   season of 1990, David _____ .
7. He slid across the plate with the elec-
   trifying run that won the 1992 pennant
   for the Braves, Sid _____ .
9. Home ballpark of the Braves,
   _____ County Stadium.
10. The Road Runner, Ralph _____ .
11. Braves' opponents in the 1991 World
    Series.
12. This Braves' outfielder led the National
    League in 1970 with a .366 batting
    average, Rico _____ .
13. This Hall of Fame pitcher won a total
    of 363 games, Warren _____ .
14. Braves' opponents in the 1957 and
    1958 World Series.
15. Catcher for the 1957 World Champion
    Milwaukee Braves, Del _____ .

19. This Hall of Fame third baseman
    played for the Braves in Boston, Mil-
    waukee and Atlanta.
21. This Hall of Fame shortstop played for
    the Boston Braves in the 1920's, Dave
    _____ .
23. This second baseman joined the
    Braves in 1973 and hit 43 homers his
    first season in Atlanta, Dave _____ .
24. He beat the pickoff attempt by Bob
    Feller in the controversial first game of
    the 1948 World Series, catcher Phil
    _____ .
26. This pitcher won 15 games with a 2.85
    ERA for the NL Champion Braves in
    1992, John _____ .
28. Braves' opponents in the 1948 World
    Series.
30. He stole 72 bases for the Braves in
    1991, Otis _____ .

33. Surprise hero of the 1992 NLCS with the game winning hit in Game 7 against the Pirates, Francisco _____ .
34. All Star centerfielder for the Boston Braves in the 1930's, Wally _____ .
35. He won 23 games for the 1969 NL West Champion Braves, knuckleballer Phil _____ .
36. 30-30 man for the Braves in 1990 and 1991, Ron _____ .
37. Hall of Fame shortstop who was part of the 1914 Miracle Braves, Rabbit ____ .

DOWN

1. This Atlanta outfielder won two straight MVP awards, Dale _____ .
2. Atlanta third baseman who became the NL Rookie of the Year in 1978, Bob _____ .
4. He won 24 games for the 1948 NL Champion Boston Braves, Johnny _____ .
5. Complete game (abbrev.).
6. This Atlanta catcher was named the National League Rookie of the Year in 1971, _____ Williams.
7. His three World Series victories led the Braves' to their 1957 World Championship, Lew _____ .
8. This Atlanta pitcher wore "Channel 17" on his uniform in 1976 as a promotion for the team owner's TV station, Andy _____ .

11. Jane Fonda's famous husband, Ted _____ .
15. First baseman for the 1982 NL West Champion Braves, Chris _____ .
16. Owner of the Boston Braves who signed an aging Babe Ruth in 1935, Judge Emil _____ .
17. Braves pitcher who belted two grand slams in a 1966 game, Tony _____ .
18. Utility infielder for the Braves in the late 1950's, Felix _____ .
20. Atlanta third baseman who blasted 41 homers in 1973, Darrell _____ .
22. A 1992 collision at home plate kept this Atlanta catcher out of postseason activity, Greg _____ .
25. He managed the Braves to pennants in 1991 and 1992, Bobby _____ .
27. This right-hander led the Braves in victories in 1973 and 1975, Carl _____ .
29. This left-hander went 18-8 for the pennant winning Braves in 1991, Steve _____ .
31. The greatest home run hitter of all time.
32. Hall of Famer who played second base for the Miracle Braves of 1914, Johnny _____ .
34. This pitcher had an 18-7 record for the 1957 World Champion Milwaukee Braves, Bob _____ .

CINCINNATI REDS

When asked to think about the Cincinnati Reds, most fans would focus on the dominant Big Red Machine of the 1970's. This offensive powerhouse, led by infielders Pete Rose, Joe Morgan, Tony Perez, and Dave Concepcion, catcher Johnny Bench, and outfielders George Foster, Ken Griffey, Sr., and Cesar Geronimo, terrorized NL pitchers for nearly a decade. Many consider this Reds group to be baseball's last great dynasty.

Rose won the NL Rookie of the Year honors in 1963 and quickly established himself as baseball's biggest overachiever, a real hustling competitor. Bench came up in 1968, and didn't disappoint. By the end of his Hall of Fame career, Bench had established himself as one of the greatest catchers in history.

Sparky Anderson took over as manager in 1970 and led the team to the World Series in his first year. This was the beginning of a decade of domination that sent the Reds to the World Series four times and produced World Championships in 1975 and 1976, as well as six divisional titles.

The 1975 World Series was a true classic and is generally regarded as instrumental to a resurgence of baseball's popularity in the 1970's. The Series pitted the Reds against the American League champion, the Boston Red Sox. One of the things that raised the stakes going into the Series was that the Reds hadn't won a championship for 35 years while the Red Sox had been waiting for 57.

The Reds and the Red Sox split the first two games. Controversy raged in Game 3. With the Reds at bat in the bottom of the tenth inning and the score tied, Ed Armbrister bunted and hesitated in the batter's box before taking off for first. This got him momentarily tangled with Boston catcher Carlton Fisk who misplayed the ball, allowing Armbrister to reach first safely. The Red Sox vehemently protested that Armbrister had interfered with Fisk, but Umpire Larry Barnett refused to call him out. This play enabled the Reds to score the winning run and take a 2-1 edge in the Series.

The Reds held a three-games-to-two lead going into Game 6, and the stage was set for the "greatest game of all time" as it has been called. Cesar Geronimo had homered in the top of the eighth inning to give the Reds a 6-3 lead, and they needed only six more outs to eliminate the Red Sox. But in the bottom of the eighth, former Cincinnati Red Bernie Carbo smacked a clutch pinch-hit three-run homer to tie the score. Fenway Park erupted in a frenzy.

The heroics continued. In the bottom of the ninth, Boston's Denny Doyle tagged up at third and raced home as George Foster caught a fly ball in left. Foster threw a perfect strike to the plate to cut down the winning run and send the game into extra innings. In the top of the eleventh, Joe Morgan hit a ball to deep right which looked to be a sure home run, but Boston's Dwight Evans made an incredible catch at the wall, then whirled and fired the ball back to the infield for a double play.

It was an emotionally drained America that watched Sox catcher Carlton Fisk step up to the plate in the bottom of the twelfth and send a Pat Darcy pitch down towards the left field foul pole, waving it fair as he ran to first, in one of baseball's most unforgettable moments.

The Big Red Machine rebounded to win Game 7 and the Series, thanks to a game-winning single by Joe Morgan in the ninth inning.

The following year, the Reds won the World Series again, this time sweeping the Yankees in four.

The Reds only championship before 1975 came in 1940. Hall of Fame manager Bill McKechnie led a line up that included catcher Ernie Lombardi, MVP Frank McCormick, and pitching aces Bucky Walters and Paul Derringer over the Detroit Tigers in seven games.

In 1984, hometown favorite Pete Rose made his triumphant return to the Reds as player-manager. The following year Rose made baseball history when he broke Ty Cobb's all-time career hit record.

Rookie Manager Lou Piniella led the Reds back to the World Series in 1990. The strong pitching of Jose Rijo and relievers Ron Dibble and Norm Charlton, and the clutch hitting of Barry Larkin, Paul O'Neill and Eric Davis paced the Reds as they topped the Pirates in the playoffs and then surprised everyone by sweeping the heavily favored Oakland A's in four games in the World Series.

Solution on page 143.

ACROSS

2. Hall of fame catcher for the Big Red Machine.

7. Shortstop for the 1990 World Champion Reds, Barry _____ .

10. Reds' shortstop throughout the seventies and eighties, Dave _____ .

12. Third baseman traded to the Dodgers in 1989, Lenny _____ .

14. This fireballer recorded 274 K's for the Reds in 1982, Mario _____ .

15. This former Indian won 12 games for the Reds in 1992, Greg _____ .

16. The Reds' new manager for 1993, Tony _____ .

17. Award for fielding excellence, the Gold _____ .

18. In the 1950's, the team was known as the Cincinnati Red _____ .

19. He pitched a perfect game against the Dodgers in 1988.

22. Third baseman for the 1990 World Champion Reds.

23. Hall of Fame outfielder for the 1919 World Champion Reds, Edd _____ .

25. This sidearm hurler for the Reds in the forties was known as "The Whip", Ewell _____ .

27. Hall of Fame catcher for the 1940 World Champion Reds, Ernie _____ .

30. This rookie outfielder batted .270 for the Reds in 1992, Reggie _____ .

32. This Cincinnati third baseman led the NL with 130 RBI in 1965, _____ Johnson.

34. He got the only World Series victory for the Reds against the 1961 Yankees, Joey _____ .

36. Centerfielder for the 1975 and 1976 World Champion Reds, Cesar _____ .

37. He managed the Reds in 1981 to the best record in the majors, John _____ .

38. River _____ Stadium.

39. Reds' home ballpark up until 1970, _____ Field.

40. First baseman for the 1970 National League Champion Reds, Lee _____ .

DOWN

1. He pitched two consecutive no-hitters in 1938, Johnny _____ Meer.

3. He pitched for the Reds at age 15 in 1944, Joe _____ .

4. He won 25 games for the 1939 National League Champion Reds, Paul _____ .

5. Manager of the 1990 World Champion Reds.

6. Rightfielder for the 1990 World Champion Reds, Paul _____ .

8. Cincinnati slugger from the 1950's, Big Ted _____ .

9. Dibble and Myers were called the _____ Boys.

10. He played short for the Reds in the 1960's, Leo _____ .

11. Reds' Hall of Fame pitcher _____ Rixey.

13. Shortstop (abbrev.).

19. This former Dodger won 15 games for the Reds in 1992, Tim _____ .

20. At the age of 19 he won 14 games for the Reds in 1967, Gary _____ .

21. 1990 World Series MVP (two words).

22. He managed the Reds to championships in 1975 and 1976, _____ Anderson.

24. This Cincinnati third baseman was named the NL Rookie of the Year in 1966, Tommy _____ .

26. Reds' All Star outfielder in 1992, _____ Roberts.

28. This Cincinnati pitching ace threw three no-hitters in the 1960's, losing one of them, Jim _____ .

29. National League MVP in 1975 and 1976, Joe _____ .

31. He blasted 37 homers and 100 RBI for the Reds in 1987, Eric _____ .

33. Charlie Hustle.

35. This outfielder batted .343 for the 1961 National League Champion Reds, _____ Pinson.

Division Finishes 1983-1992

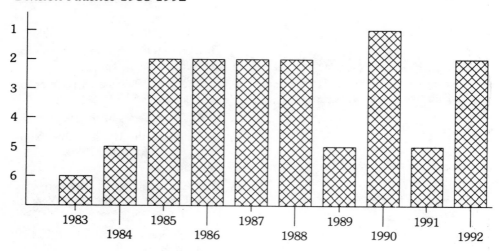

League Leaders 1983-1992

Category	Year	Leader	
RBI	1985	Dave Parker	125
Doubles		Dave Parker	42
Rookie of the Year	1988	Chris Sabo	
Wins		Danny Jackson	23 (T)
Saves		John Franco	39
Triples	1990	Mariano Duncan	11
Winning Pct.	1991	Jose Rijo	.714 (15-6) (T)

1992 Leaders

Category	Player	
Batting Average	Bip Roberts	.323
Home Runs	Paul O'Neill	14
RBI	Barry Larkin	78
Stolen Bases	Bip Roberts	44
Doubles	Bip Roberts	34
Triples	Reggie Sanders	6 (T)
	Bip Roberts	6 (T)
	Barry Larkin	6 (T)
Runs	Bip Roberts	92
Hits	Bip Roberts	172
Wins	Tim Belcher	15 (T)
	Jose Rijo	15 (T)
ERA	Jose Rijo	2.56
Strikeouts	Jose Rijo	171
Saves	Norm Charlton	26

HOUSTON ASTROS

During the 1950's, baseball experienced a geographical shakeup. Several teams had pulled up their stakes and moved, in some cases cross-country, and the game received an injection of new interest from fans in cities that had never before seen Mickey Mantle hit a homer or Willie Mays steal a base.

One person who took note of this phenomenon was the venerable Branch Rickey, astute as ever in his late seventies. In 1959, he hatched a plan for a new major league, the Continental League, to fill the void in cities that were willing and able to support a major league team.

The National and American Leagues didn't care for this idea at all and decided to combat it by offering the choicest of Rickey's prospective team owners a chance to join the established leagues as an expansion team. One of the prospective team owners was Judge Roy Hofheinz of Houston.

The National League finally expanded in 1962, and the Houston team, called the Colt .45's, joined the league along with the New York Mets. The two teams seemed to have different agendas from the outset, as evidenced by the expansion draft.

The Mets had to compete with the Yankees tin New York. Their plan was to attract former Giant and Dodger fans. They chose to draft a number of aging, big-name players for their gate appeal rather than build for the future.

Under the direction of general manager Paul Richards, an accomplished evaluator of baseball talent, the Colt's selected younger players with potential. Joe Morgan, Jim Wynn, Rusty Staub, Jerry Grote and Dave Giusti are all players developed by Houston in the early sixties.

Although they consistently outperformed the hapless Mets, they never finished higher than eighth in the old ten-team league. The team also found that playing baseball outdoors in Houston could be a miserable experience for players and fans alike because of the sweltering heat and giant mosquitoes.

Fortunately, Hofheinz realized this and built an indoor stadium, the Astrodome, which opened in 1965. The first structure of its kind, the Astrodome was touted as the eighth wonder of the world by its many admirers. The structure was the pioneer of indoor baseball and artificial surfaces, both integral parts of today's game, though baseball purists may disagree.

The franchise now known as the Astros took awhile to gel as a team. They flirted with pennant fever in the tight five-team NL West race in 1969 but didn't become serious contenders until ten years later.

In 1979, the Astros rose to the top almost exclusively with pitching. Led by Joe Niekro, J.R. Richard, and bullpen stopper Joe Sambito, they made-up for their usual light offense and finished second in the NL West, just one and one-half games out of first.

The following year, the team added veterans Nolan Ryan and Joe Morgan who helped lead the Astros to their first division title. It didn't come easily, and the Astros nearly let it slip away at the end. Holding a three game lead with three to play, they lost three games to the Dodgers in LA to force a one-game playoff. Fortunately, Niekro saved the season with a superb 7-1 victory in the tie-breaker.

Newcomers to postseason play, the Astros locked horns with the Phillies in the 1980 NLCS, one of the most exciting playoffs of all time. Four of the five games went into extra innings, and Game 5 was the ultimate nail-biter as the lead changed several times before the Phillies finally prevailed in the tenth to take the series and the pennant.

In the strike year of 1981, the Astros came on strong at the end to take the second-half pennant but were downed by the Dodgers in the divisional playoffs, as LA's Jerry Reuss pitched a shutout in the fifth and final contest.

The Astros reached the playoffs again in 1986, thanks to great pitching by Mike Scott and the strong offensive performances of Glenn Davis and Kevin Bass. They were to come out on the short end again of a tremendously exciting playoff series, as they lost to the Mets in six games despite the brilliance of Scott who was named the Most Valuable Player of the NLCS.

In 1992, the Astros were one of baseball's biggest surprises. They finished with an 81-81 record despite some formidable obstacles, most notably a grueling 26-game road trip caused by the Republican National Convention being held at the Astrodome during the summer. They also endured owner John McMullen's apparent indifference toward building a winning team, as evidenced by his desire to keep the team's payroll as low as possible.

In 1993, the Astros suddenly look like contenders again. They have a new owner, a solid young nucleus of players, and a pitching staff bolstered by the signings of free agents Doug Drabek and Greg Swindell.

Division Finishes 1983-1992

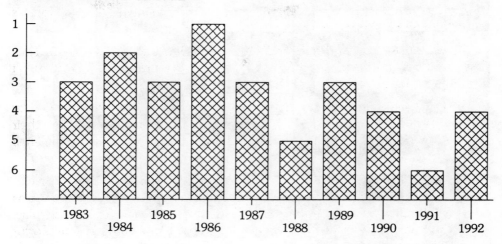

League Leaders 1983-1992

Category	Year	Leader	
Hits	1983	Jose Cruz	189 (T)
Cy Young	1986	Mike Scott	
ERA		Mike Scott	2.22
Strikeouts		Mike Scott	306
ERA	1987	Nolan Ryan	2.76
Strikeouts		Nolan Ryan	270
Strikeouts	1988	Nolan Ryan	228
Wins	1989	Mike Scott	20
ERA	1990	Danny Darwin	2.21
Rookie of the Year	1991	Jeff Bagwell	

1992 Leaders

Category	Player	
Batting Average	Ken Caminiti	.294
Home Runs	Eric Anthony	19
RBI	Jeff Bagwell	96
Stolen Bases	Steve Finley	44
Doubles	Jeff Bagwell	34
Triples	Steve Finley	177
Runs	Craig Biggio	96
Hits	Steve Finley	13
Wins	Doug Jones	11
ERA	Pete Harnisch	3.70
Strikeouts	Pete Harnisch	164
Saves	Doug Jones	36

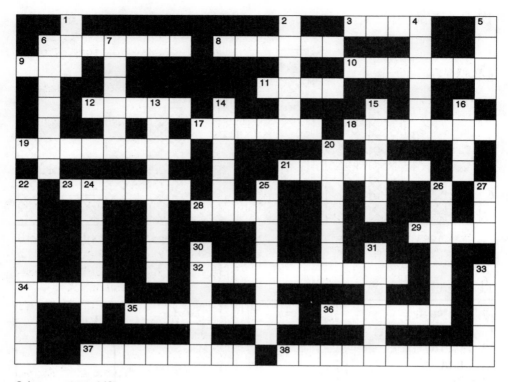

Solution on page 143.

ACROSS

3. They couldn't grow grass indoors, so the Astros started using artificial ____ .

6. He led the Astros in homers and RBI in his rookie year of 1991, Jeff ____ .

8. Third baseman for the 1980 NL West Champion Astros, Enos ____ .

9. This first baseman knocked in 105 runs for the Astros in 1973, Lee ____ .

10. Mainstay of the early Houston pitching staff, Turk ____ .

11. Houston's 1962 expansion partners.

12. This left-hander led Astro pitchers in saves in 1991 with 12, Al ____ .

17. He managed the 1980 Western Division Champion Astros, Bill ____ .

18. Astro pitching great who suffered a stroke in 1980, ending his career, J.R. ____ .

19. The Astros' regular third baseman since 1989, Ken ____ .

21. In 1969 he became the Astros' first 20 game winner, Larry ____ .

23. This reliever posted a 9-1 record for Houston in 1992, ____ Hernandez.

28. He became the Astros' manager in 1989.

29. The Astros traded him to the Mets for Mike Scott, Danny ____ .

32. This former American league slugger player for the Astros in 1992, Pete ____ .

34. This shortstop stole 49 bases as an Astro rookie in 1966, ____ Jackson.

35. Astros' opponents in the memorable 1980 NLCS.

36. Houston manager from 1968 to 1972, Harry "The Hat" ____ .

37. In 1991, he led Astro pitchers with 12 wins and 172 strikeouts, Pete ____ .

38. Before 1965 the team was known as the Colt _____ .

DOWN

1. This Astro reliever "stung" opposing batters while chalking up a 10-4 mark in 1971, Jim _____ .
2. Centerfielder for the 1980 NL West Champion Astros, Cesar _____ .
4. He pitched a no-hitter against the Braves in 1979, Ken _____ .
5. He finished up the 1992 season with an impressive 11-strikeout performance against the Dodgers, Darryl _____ .
6. Astro catcher from the sixties, John _____ .
7. As a rookie in 1967 he no-hit the Braves, Don _____ .
13. He tossed a no-hitter against Philadelphia in 1963, Don _____ .
14. Catcher turned second baseman, Craig _____ .

15. He won 20 in helping the Astros to the 1980 NL West crown, Joe _____ .
16. Astro outfielder from 1975 to 1987, Jose _____ .
20. Led the Astros with 64 stolen bases in 1990, Eric _____ .
22. Catcher for the both the 1980 and 1986 NL West Champion Astros, (two words).
24. Houston outfielder who knocked in 80 runs in 1992, Eric _____ .
25. This left-hander posted a 12-5 record for the 1986 Astros, Jim _____ .
26. This left-hander posted a 17-12 record for the 1986 Astros, Bob _____ .
27. This political party held their convention in the Astrodome in 1992.
30. He was the shortstop on Houston's 1962 expansion club, Bob _____ .
31. Astro centerfielder who batted .292 in 1992, Steve _____ .
33. The power hitter on the 1986 Astros, first baseman Glenn _____ .

LOS ANGELES DODGERS

Los Angeles Dodgers - last place, National League West, 1992.

For the Dodger faithful, the 1992 season was the worst in memory. The Dodgers have not finished in last place since 1905. Their history is loaded with baseball successes and charismatic characters.

The Brooklyn Dodgers rode atop the NL in the late forties and early fifties. From 1947 to 1956, they won six NL pennants, one world championship, and lost the pennant on the last day of the season two other times. They were the "Boys of Summer" and are remembered now as representatives of baseball in a simpler time, romanticized as heroes of the Borough of Brooklyn. The Dodgers were a big part of Brooklyn's identity. This made it all the more painful when owner Walter O'Malley pulled the Dodgers from the city.

The Brooklyn Dodgers peaked in 1955 when they won their first and only World Series, beating the New York Yankees, who had frustrated them so many times before. The Dodgers actually lost the first two games of the '55 Series, but, thanks to the pitching of Johnny Podres and an unforgettable catch by Sandy Amoros, they hung on to take the Series in seven.

Baseball fever in Brooklyn can be traced back as far as 1870, when baseball's first professional team, the Cincinnati Red Stockings, travelled the land, beating everybody in sight. Everybody, that is, until they took on the Brooklyn Atlantics on June 14 of that year.

The Cincinnati nine were riding a 92 game winning streak. Fanatical Brooklyn fans cheered their team on its way to ending the longest winning streak in baseball history. Legend has it that Dodger fans did more than cheer, actually. One fan jumped a Cincinnati outfielder chasing a fly ball.

The first Brooklyn pennant of the twentieth century came in 1916. That year they lost four out of five to Babe Ruth and the Red Sox in the World Series. Four years later they again made the World Series, this time losing a wild and woolly affair to Tris Speaker and the Cleveland Indians.

In the twenties, the team had little on-field success, but their charisma was starting to take shape. They became known as the "Daffiness Boys," a synonym for lovable losers that the Mets would play to perfection four decades later.

116

It's not that there weren't any good players on the team. In the twenties, Brooklyn teams featured Dazzy Vance, Burleigh Grimes, Zach Wheat, Max Carey, and Manager Wilbert Robinson, all Hall of Famers. During the thirties and forties, the Dodgers had Babe Herman, Van Lingle Mungo and Dixie Walker.

Branch Rickey is given credit for assembling the great Dodger teams of the forties and fifties and breaking baseball's color barrier in 1947 by signing Jackie Robinson to the team. Walter O'Malley replaced Rickey as Dodger president in 1950. These men put together the Dodger teams that featured such well known names as Robinson, Duke Snider, Pee Wee Reese, Gil Hodges, Roy Campanella, Don Newcombe, Carl Furillo, Carl Erskine, and Preacher Roe. Campanella may have been the best of this fabled group, winning three MVP awards before his career was cut short by a tragic auto accident that left him paralyzed.

After the team moved to Los Angeles, they consistently stood among baseball's top teams and captured several championships along the way to becoming the biggest financial success in the history of baseball.

The Dodgers took the title in their second year in LA, defeating the White Sox in the 1959 World Series. They smashed Series attendance records that year because they were playing their games in the enormous LA Coliseum. Their three home games averaged an amazing 92,000 fans per game.

The Dodgers of the sixties won three pennants and two World Series led mainly by the pitching strength of Sandy Koufax and Don Drysdale and the speed of Maury Wills. From 1961 to his peak in 1966, Koufax was the best pitcher in baseball and maybe the best ever. Unfortunately, arm problems forced a premature end to his career. Drysdale is best remembered for his 58 scoreless inning streak of 1968, a record until another Dodger, Orel Hershiser, broke it in 1988.

The Dodgers participated in three World Series in the seventies but were defeated each time by a Reggie Jackson-led team. In 1974, Jackson led his Oakland A's over the Dodgers in five. In 1977 and 1978, he led the Yankees to back to back championships. In fact, it was mainly at the expense of the Dodgers that Jackson earned the name "Mr. October."

The Dodgers got their revenge in 1981 with a World Series victory over the Yankees, led by co-MVP's Pedro Guerrero, Steve Yeager, and Ron Cey.

Orel Hershiser and Kirk Gibson led the Dodgers to another championship in 1988. Hershiser mesmerized NL batters throughout his Cy Young Award winning season, then did the same to Oakland batters in the World Series where he was named MVP. Gibson won the NL MVP award but batted only once in the Series because he was sidelined by leg injuries. Facing Oakland relief ace Dennis Eckersley, Gibson smacked a pinch homer and hobbled around the bases. Gibson's heroic appearance inspired the Dodgers to a four-one Series victory over the A's, making them the only team to win two world championships in the 1980's.

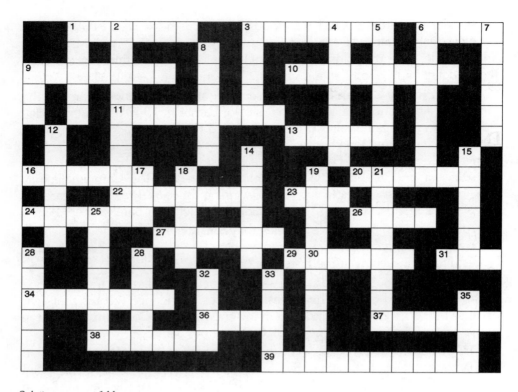

Solution on page 144.

ACROSS

1. Site of Dodger Stadium, Chavez _____ .

3. Long time Dodger shortstop who retired in 1986, Bill _____ .

6. Baseball's greatest pinch hitter, Manny _____ .

9. 1941 NL MVP who led the Dodgers to the pennant, Dolph _____ .

10. Dodger catcher who was hit over the head with Juan Marichal's bat.

11. Kevin Gross pitched one of these against the Giants on August 17, 1992.

13. This Hall of Famer led the NL in strikeouts for seven consecutive years (1922-1928), Dazzy _____ .

16. He shut out the Yankees in Game 7 of the 1955 World Series to give the Dodgers their first championship.

20. The Duke of Flatbush.

22. Dodger manager since 1977.

23. This Dodger relief specialist had 28 saves in 1989 with a 1.58 ERA, _____ Howell.

24. This Dodger ace won three Cy Young Awards - in 1963, 1965, and 1966.

26. His passed ball in the 1941 World Series will live in infamy, Mickey _____ .

27. His collision with an outfield wall in 1942 shortened a promising career, Pete _____ .

30. He had an outstanding year as the Dodgers' rookie first baseman in 1992, Eric _____ .

31. This left-hander posted a 16-12 record for the 1977 Dodgers with a 2.57 ERA, Doug _____ .

34. Dodger President, Peter _____ .

36. He threw 59 straight scoreless innings in 1988, _____ Hershiser.

37. Home of the Brooklyn Dodgers, _____ Field.

38. His big win in Game 3 of the 1965 World Series over the Twins got the Dodgers on track to a championship, Claude _____ .

39. The Dodgers' 1992 All Star representative, Mike _____ .

DOWN

1. He went 20-6 for the Dodgers in 1990, _____ Martinez.

2. Dodger hurler who won the Cy Young Award in 1981.

3. Hall of Fame shortstop, Pee Wee _____ .

4. He went 20-6 for the Dodgers in 1953, Carl _____ .

5. Dodger relief ace in the '50's, Clem _____ .

6. This Hall of Famer was a member of Brooklyn's pennant-winning pitching staffs in 1916 and 1920, Rube _____ .

7. Dodger manager from 1954 to 1976, Walter _____ .

8. He struck out 209 as a Dodger rookie in 1966, Don _____ .

9. Brooklyn's slick fielding third baseman of the 1950's, Billy _____ .

12. His catch of a ball hit by Yogi Berra in Game 7 of the 1955 World Series saved the game, Sandy _____ .

14. Dodger catcher from 1972 to 1985, Steve _____ .

15. He served up the fateful homerun pitch to Bobby Thomson on October 3, 1951, Ralph _____ .

17. 1982 NL Rookie of the Year, Steve _____ .

18. NL stolen base leader in 1975 and 1976, Davey _____ .

19. This Dodger catcher was a three-time MVP, Roy _____ .

21. The first-ever Cy Young Award was given out in 1956, and he won it, Don _____ .

25. This Dodger outfielder was known as the Reading Rifle, Carl _____ .

28. His knuckle curve stopped the Yankees in Game 7 of the 1981 World Series, Burt _____ .

29. Brooklyn left fielder from 1909 to 1926, Hall of Famer Zach _____ .

32. Left fielder for the 1959 World Champion Dodgers, Wally _____ .

33. This Dodger speedster stole 104 bases in 1962, Maury _____ .

35. His playoff victory against the Braves in 1959 won the pennant for the Dodgers, _____ Williams.

Division Finishes 1983-1992

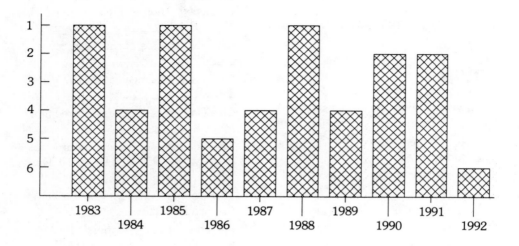

League Leaders 1983-1992

Category	Year	Leader	
ERA	1984	Alejandro Pena	2.48
Winning Pct.	1985	Orel Hershiser	.864 (19-3)
Wins	1986	Fernando Valenzuela	21
MVP	1988	Kirk Gibson	
Cy Young		Orel Hershiser	
Wins		Orel Hershiser	23 (T)
Runs	1991	Brett Butler	112
Rookie of the Year	1992	Eric Karros	

1992 Leaders

Category	Player	
Batting Average	Brett Butler	.309
Home Runs	Eric Karros	20
RBI	Eric Karros	88
Stolen Bases	Brett Butler	41
Doubles	Eric Karros	30
Triples	Brett Butler	11
Runs	Brett Butler	86
Hits	Brett Butler	171
Wins	Tom Candiotti	11
ERA	Tom Candiotti	3.00
Strikeouts	Kevin Gross	158
Saves	Roger McDowell	14

SAN DIEGO PADRES

The Padres, while never achieving the ultimate success of a world championship in their twenty-four year history, have at least made it to the World Series, something that five of baseball's other expansion teams cannot say. In fact, the Padres eventually recovered well from their rough beginnings which saw the team finish last their first six seasons and nearly become the third major league baseball franchise to die a slow death in our nation's capital.

The Padres entered the National League in 1969 and lost 110 games their first season under manager Preston Gomez. Their early batting stars included Nate Colbert, Cito Gaston and Downtown Ollie Brown. Colbert was a three-time National League All Star and, in 1972, enjoyed his best year as he blasted 38 homers and 111 RBI.

As with any expansion team, the pitching corps got less than their share of offensive support. The Padres were no exception. Clay Kirby and Steve Arlin were two young pitchers who performed admirably during the early days and probably deserved a better fate.

After the 1973 season, the Padres' poor performances on the field and at the gate prompted their owner to sell the team. Baseball Commissioner Bowie Kuhn was particularly hot on the idea of bringing baseball back to Washington, a city from which two franchises had previously bolted and eagerly supported the efforts of a potential buyer who wanted to move the Padres there.

It seemed so certain they would become the Washington Padres that the 1974 edition of Topps baseball cards had Washington instead of San Diego on the Padres' cards. At the last minute, entrepreneur Ray Kroc, the founder of McDonald's, stepped forward and bought the team. Kroc kept the team in San Diego.

In 1975, led by manager John McNamara, the Padres finally escaped the cellar, spurred by the performances of veteran Willie McCovey and a young outfielder named Dave Winfield. They also found a pitching gem in left-hander Randy Jones, who baffled National League hitters with his sinkerball and became the first Padre pitcher to win 20 games. The following year Jones posted a 22-14 record and captured the NL Cy Young Award.

A brilliant trade with Texas in 1978 brought the services of future Hall of Famer Gaylord Perry to San Diego. Perry went 21-6 his first season, and became the second Padre in three years to capture the Cy Young Award. About this time, the Padres began venturing into the free agent market, luring former A's Rollie Fingers and Gene Tenace to join homegrown players like Winfield and shortstop Ozzie Smith. Still, the best they finished was in fourth place. San Diego eventually lost Winfield through free agency to the New York Yankees, a major setback for the club.

In the early eighties, under new general manager Jack (Trader Jack) McKeon, the Padres began to piece together the team that would become the National League Champions in 1984. Once again, they tapped the free agent market and acquired proven winners like Graig Nettles, Steve Garvey and Goose Gossage. They also developed some star players of their own in pitchers Eric Show and Mark Thurmond, and outfielders Tony Gwynn and Kevin McReynolds.

Manager Dick Williams' 1984 squad breezed through the NL West, winning the division by 12 games. In the NLCS, their opponents were the Chicago Cubs, who, like the Padres, were making their first appearance in the playoffs.

The Series started off badly for the Padres. The Cubs beat them 13-0 in Game 1. After a tough 4-2 loss in the second game, the Padres returned to San Diego with the undesirable task of playing three "must win" games.

Nobody seemed to give the Padres much of a chance. Most of America was pulling for the Cubs to win their first pennant since 1945. Undaunted, the Padres rose to the occasion and beat the Cubs three straight times for the National League Championship.

In doing so, they became the first team to come back in the NLCS from a two games to none deficit. The Padres provided some classic baseball moments en route to victory. Garvey won Game 4 with a dramatic ninth inning homer, and the Padres capitalized on an error by Cub first baseman Leon Durham in Game 5 to pin Rick Sutcliffe with only his second Cub loss of the season.

In the World Series, however, the Padres could do little against the powerful Detroit Tigers. San Diego went quietly in five games.

Since their pennant winning 1984 season, the Padres have gone through numerous managerial changes and are still trying to find the right combination to take them back to the top.

San Diego certainly doesn't lack talent. Outfielder Tony Gwynn consistently proves himself to be the best hitter in the National League, having won four batting titles in the eighties. Reliever Mark Davis distinguished his brief stay in San Diego by winning the Cy Young Award in 1989. Fred McGriff and Gary Sheffield came to the Padres from the American League and have quickly established themselves as two of the National League's biggest stars. In 1992, McGriff led the NL in homeruns and Sheffield was in the news all year as he pursued the Triple Crown.

Division Finishes 1983-1992

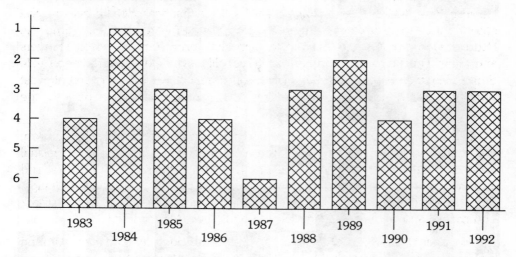

League Leaders 1983-1992

Category	Year	Leader	
Batting Average	1984	Tony Gwynn	.351
Hits		Tony Gwynn	213
Runs	1986	Tony Gwynn	107 (T)
Hits		Tony Gwynn	211
Rookie of the Year	1987	Benito Santiago	
Batting Average		Tony Gwynn	.370
Hits		Tony Gwynn	218
Batting Average	1988	Tony Gwynn	.313
Cy Young	1989	Mark Davis	
Batting Average		Tony Gwynn	.336
Saves		Mark Davis	44
Hits		Tony Gwynn	203
Batting Average	1992	Gary Sheffield	.330
Home Runs		Fred McGriff	35

1992 Leaders

Category	Player	
Batting Average	Gary Sheffield	.330
Home Runs	Fred McGriff	35
RBI	Fred McGriff	104
Stolen Bases	Tony Fernandez	20
Doubles	Gary Sheffield	34
Triples	Jerald Clark	6
Runs	Gary Sheffield	87
Hits	Gary Sheffield	184
Wins	Bruce Hurst	14
ERA	Andy Benes	3.35
Strikeouts	Andy Benes	169
Saves	Randy Myers	38

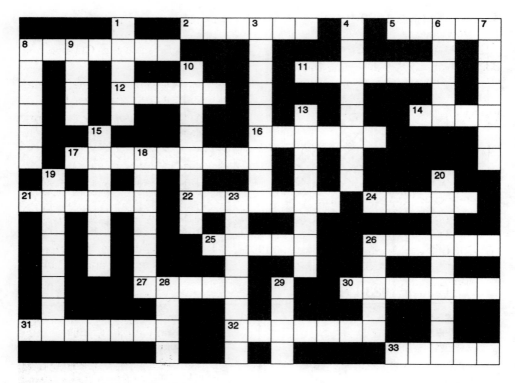

Solution on page 144.

ACROSS

2. Padre infielder acquired from New York in 1991, Tim _____ .

5. In the 1984 World Series the Padres played their away games at _____ Stadium.

8. This relief ace won 10 and saved 25 for the Padres on the way to their 1984 NL Championship.

11. This Hall of Fame slugger played for the Padres from 1974 to 1976, Willie _____ .

12. Ace reliever for the Padres in 1989 who jumped to Kansas City, Mark _____ .

14. Padre shortstop from the 70's, _____ Hernandez.

16. This knuckleballer toiled for the Padres in their first season of 1969, going 8 and 17, Joe _____ .

17. This Padre third baseman flirted with the triple crown in 1992, Gary _____ .

21. Now the manager of the World Champion Blue Jays, he was an All Star outfielder for the Padres in their early days.

22. This Padre reliever was the National League Rookie of the Year in 1976, Butch _____ .

24. The Padres' first manager, Preston _____ .

25. Former Bosox pitching ace signed by as a free agent by the Padres in 1988, Bruce _____ .

26. Home of the Padres, Jack _____ Stadium.

27. This left-handed pitcher led the Padres in strikeouts in 1976, Brent _____ .

30. Catcher for the 1984 NL Champion Padres, Terry _____ .

31. The biggest offensive star for the early Padres, Nate _____ .

32. He brought over some championship experience to the 1984 Padres, third baseman Craig _____ .
33. He won 15 games for the Padres in 1991, right-hander Andy _____ .

DOWN

1. This Padre pitcher won the Cy Young Award in 1976, _____ Jones.
3. He played short for the Padres in 1992 and batted .275, Tony _____ .
4. This Padre outfielder led the National League in triples in 1981, Gene ____ .
6. One of the NL's greatest hitters with a lifetime average of .327 through 1992, Tony _____ .
7. He was fired as Padre manager in 1992, Greg _____ .
8. First baseman for the 1984 NL Champion Padres, Steve _____ .
9. He won 15 games for the NL Champion Padres in 1964, Eric _____ .
10. The 1984 Padres were his fourth World Series team, manager Dick ___ .

13. This reliever got the key victories in Games 4 and 5 of the Padres' 1984 comeback against the Cubs in the NLCS, Craig _____ .
15. This pitcher flopped with the Yankees but was a star for the Padres, Ed ____ .
18. This Hall of Famer was the Padres' bullpen ace from 1977 to 1980, Rollie _____ .
19. This Padre catcher highlighted his 1987 rookie season with a 34-game hitting streak, Benito _____ .
20. Shortstop for the 1984 NL Champion Padres, Garry _____ .
23. This left-hander won 14 games for the 1984 NL Champion Padres, Mark _____ .
26. 1992 Padre relief ace, Randy _____ .
28. This former Giant infielder played for the Padres in the mid-seventies, _____ Fuentes.
29. The Padres traded Kevin McReynolds to the _____ in 1986 for Kevin Mitchell.

SAN FRANCISCO GIANTS

The history of the Giants in the National League dates back to 1883 when they moved from Troy, NY to New York City. The pre-1900 Giant teams featured Hall of Famers first baseman Roger Connor, catcher Buck Ewing, shortstop John Montgomery Ward, and pitchers Mickey Welch, Tim Keefe, and Amos Rusie.

In 1902, the Giants pulled a coup by signing John McGraw away from the new American League. McGraw had earned a reputation as a tough, no-nonsense player with the Baltimore Orioles of the 1890's, and his presence in the Giant dugout was instrumental in transforming the Giants into baseball's most dominant team for the next quarter century.

The Giants won the NL pennant in 1904 but refused to meet the AL Champion Boston Pilgrims in what would have been the second World Series. McGraw and Giants owner John T. Brush so resented the upstart league that they completely ignored popular sentiment and no Series was played.

McGraw's team repeated as NL champs the next year and, this time, agreed to meet the AL champion Philadelphia Athletics in a best of seven series. The Giants won the series four games to one. Each of the five games was a shutout. Giants hurler Christy Mathewson shut out the A's three times, a record that still stands. Iron Man Joe McGinnity threw the other Giant shutout, and the A's Chief Bender added a shutout of his own for the A's lone victory.

The Giants won four consecutive pennants from 1921 to 1924. The first two of those years, they took the World Series from the new and improved Yankees who now had the services of Babe Ruth. The 1921 and 1922 Series involved no travel, because both teams called the Polo Grounds home. These were the only two same state, same city, same stadium championships.

In 1923, the Yankees built their own ballpark in the Bronx and defeated their former landlords in that year's World Series, winning their first championship. In 1924, the Giants lost their second Series in a row to the upstart Washington Senators, thanks to a couple of fluke plays in the twelfth inning of the seventh game.

John McGraw finally called it quits in 1932. The Giants named Bill Terry the new manager. Under Terry, the Giants won pennants in 1933, 1936 and 1937.

126

The Giants rebounded in 1951 with one of the most memorable late-season comebacks in baseball history. The Dodgers appeared to be cruising to their third pennant in five years, holding a 13 1/2 game lead over the Giants in mid-August. Led by outfielder Monte Irvin and pitchers Sal Maglie and Larry Jansen, the Gothams refused to give up. Rookie Willie Mays provided an additional spark to help the Giants catch the Dodgers at season's end.

The tie at season's end forced a three game playoff to decide the pennant winner. The Dodgers took a 4-1 lead into the 9th inning of Game 3 but couldn't hold it. Dodger Ralph Branca served up the pitch that Bobby Thomson clouted for the "Shot Heard Round the World." Thomson's home run rocked the Polo Grounds into hysteria, but the euphoria lasted only until the following afternoon when the Giants were faced with the AL champion Yankees. The Yankees proved too tough, and put the Giants away in six games.

In 1954, the Giants took the pennant again, largely thanks to a super year by Mays, who was starting to emerge as one of baseball's greats. This year they faced the powerful Cleveland Indians in the World Series and shocked them with a four-game sweep, thanks to Mays' unbelievable catch in Game 1 and the clutch pinch hitting of Dusty Rhodes.

The Giants left New York after the season of 1957 for the greener pastures of San Francisco and soon started to build a contending club around Mays and newcomers Orlando Cepeda, Willie McCovey, Felipe Alou and Juan Marichal. In 1962, they took the NL crown, once again defeating the Dodgers in a three-game playoff but, once again, losing to the Yankees in the World Series.

Since the advent of divisional play, the Giants have made it to the playoffs three times. They went no further than the NLCS in 1971 and 1987, but in 1989 the Giants finally made it back to the fall classic.

Unfortunately for the Giants, their tragedies in 1989 will probably be remembered more than their triumphs. Pitcher Dave Dravecky made a remarkable comeback from a cancerous tumor in his pitching arm only to fall and break the arm two starts later while throwing a pitch. Then, in the Series, as the Giants and the A's were set to start Game 3, a devastating earthquake hit the Bay area. Candlestick Park shook, terrifying the sellout crowd. The game was postponed. After a ten-day period of dealing with the tragedy, Commissioner Fay Vincent ordered play to resume. The A's promptly completed their four game sweep of the Giants.

Giants fans went through a lot in 1992. Frustrated by the city of San Francisco's repeated refusal to build a new stadium, owner Bob Lurie announced during the 1992 season that he had sold the Giants, and they were moving to the Tampa-St. Petersburg area for the 1993 season. Baseball owners blocked the move and forced Lurie to sell the team to a group that promised to keep the Giants in San Francisco. The new owners immediately made big news by signing baseball's most sought after player, Barry Bonds.

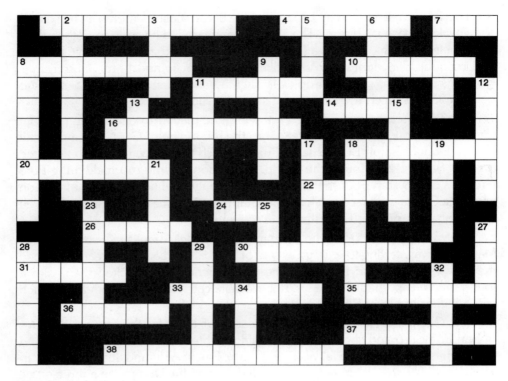

Solution on page 144.

ACROSS

1. He covered third base for the Giants in the sixties, Jim _____ .

4. The pinch hitter for the Giants who became the hero of the 1954 World Series, Dusty _____ .

7. This Giant Hall of Famer hit 511 career home runs, Mel _____ .

8. 1989 marked the career year for this Giant slugger, Kevin _____ .

10. Relief ace for the 1962 National League champion Giants, Stu _____ .

11. This Giant hurler won 24 games in 1973, Ron _____ .

14. Hall of Fame first baseman for the Giants in the 1920's, George "_____ Pockets" Kelly.

16. This Hall of Fame pitcher was known as Big Six, Christy _____ .

18. This knuckleballer began his long career with the 1952 New York Giants, Hoyt _____ .

20. He tossed a no-hitter against the Mets in 1975, Ed _____ .

22. Arm trouble has slowed the career of this 1983 Giant All Star pitcher, _____ Hammaker.

24. He won 23 games for the 1951 NL Champion New York Giants, _____ Maglie.

26. Manager of the 1989 NL Champion San Francisco Giants.

30. This turn-of-the-century Giant catcher was the first to wear shin guards, Hall of Famer Roger _____ .

31. What Tony Bennett left in San Francisco.

33. The Giants' "Meal Ticket" of the 1930's, Hall of Fame pitcher Carl_____ .

35. He won 24 games for the 1962 NL Champion Giants, Jack _____ .

36. Former Seattle hurler who won 10 and lost 4 for the Giants in 1992, Bill __ .

37. Relief ace for the Giants in the late seventies, Gary _____ .

38. Home of the SF Giants since 1960, _____ Park.

DOWN

2. He won 21 games for the 1954 World Champion New York Giants, Johnny _____ .

3. Home ballpark of the Giants when they played in New York, the _____ Grounds.

5. Giant slugger from the sixties, Jim Ray _____ .

6. This pre-1900 Hall of Famer was considered baseball's greatest catcher, Buck _____ .

7. This left-hander won 19 games for the 1962 NL Champion Giants, Billy __ .

8. Hall of Fame pitching ace for the Giants in the 1960's, Juan _____ .

9. He led the Giants with 13 wins in their division winning season of 1987, Mike _____ .

11. Popular catcher for the Giants in the eighties, Bob _____ .

12. He managed the Giants during the sixties, _____ Franks.

13. Manager of the 1962 NL Champion Giants, Al _____ .

15. This SF second baseman belted a grand slam in the 1962 World Series, Chuck _____ .

17. Hall of Fame Giant shortstop from the 1920's, _____ Jackson.

18. He blasted 34 homers for the Giants in 1991, Matt _____ .

19. He played third for the Giants from 1976 to 1983, Darrell _____ .

21. This Hall of Famer led the Giant attack in 1951 with 124 runs batted in, Monte _____ .

23. Legendary Giant manager from 1902 to 1932, John _____ .

25. The owner of the Giants from 1976 to 1992, Bob _____ .

27. Hall of Fame pitcher/shortstop from the 1880's, John Montgomery _____ .

28. First baseman for the 1954 World Champion Giants, _____ Lockman.

29. He was a Giant slugger in the 1920's while his brother Bob played for the Yankees, Irish _____ .

32. Bobby Thomson hit the shot heard round the _____ .

34. This former Astro outfielder played for the Giants from 1990-1992, Kevin _____ .

Division Finishes 1983-1992

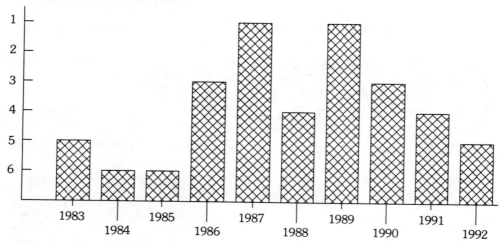

League Leaders 1983-1992

Category	Year	Leader	
ERA	1983	Atlee Hammaker	2.25
RBI	1988	Will Clark	109
Runs		Brett Butler	109
MVP	1989	Kevin Mitchell	
ERA		Scott Garrelts	2.28
Home Runs		Kevin Mitchell	47
RBI		Kevin Mitchell	125
Triples		Robby Thompson	11
Runs		Will Clark	104 (T)
RBI	1990	Matt Williams	122
Hits		Brett Butler	192 (T)
ERA	1992	Bill Swift	2.08

1992 Leaders

Category	Player	
Batting Average	Will Clark	.300
Home Runs	Matt Williams	20
RBI	Will Clark	73
Stolen Bases	Darren Lewis	28
Doubles	Will Clark	40
Triples	Matt Williams	5 (T)
	Kirt Manwaring	5 (T)
Runs	Will Clark	69
Hits	Will Clark	154
Wins	John Burkett	13
ERA	Bill Swift	3.35
Strikeouts	John Burkett	107
Saves	Rod Beck	17

EXPANSION TEAMS

The National League's 1993 expansion marks baseball's first since the American League added the Toronto Blue Jays and Seattle Mariners in 1977.

On November 17, 1992 the expansion draft was held in New York City and the new teams, the Florida Marlins and the Colorado Rockies, stocked up with players before a nationally televised audience. The first players chosen were Atlanta Brave pitcher David Nied by the Colorado Rockies and outfielder Nigel Wilson by the Marlins from the World Champion Blue Jays.

For the first time in expansion draft history, the new clubs were able to choose from teams in both leagues. While many of the players chosen were minor leaguers, there were a few big name surprises.

Bryan Harvey, the California Angels reliever, was selected by the Marlins in the first round. This was a shock not only because of his high salary ($3.8 million), but also because he missed much of 1992 with an arm injury. In another questionable move, the Yankees elected to leave their starting third baseman Charlie Hayes unprotected, and he was quickly grabbed by the Rockies as the third overall pick.

There are many questions to be answered during the 1993 season: Will the high altitude in Denver cause home runs to fly out of Mile High Stadium in record numbers? Will the moist, tropical air in southern Florida have the opposite effect on fly balls? Can the Marlin's Orestes Destrade match Cecil Fielder's success as a veteran of the Japanese League? And finally, can either team possibly entertain hopes of being in a pennant race?

One thing is certain, the 1993 season won't be dull.

COLORADO ROCKIES

Solution on page 145.

ACROSS

1. Left-handed pitcher who went 6-9 for the Astros in 1992, Butch _____ .

3. Nickname of Denver's Triple-A minor league team from 1955 to 1985.

5. The Rockies' first manager, Don _____ .

8. Colorado's general manager, Bob___ .

9. This Colorado catcher batted .270 for the Cubs in 1992, Joe _____ .

13. Colorado first baseman, a former Expo and Cardinal, Andres _____ .

14. The Rockies acquired this outfielder from Milwaukee in a trade for Kevin Reimer, _____ Bichette.

18. He pitched for Denver in 1981 and was named the American Association Pitcher of the Year. Now he's a Rockie, Bryn _____ .

20. Right-handed pitcher drafted from the Phillies' roster, Andy _____ .

21. Rockies' first base coach who caught two perfect games during his major league career, Ron _____ .

22. Long-time major league skipper who got his managerial start in Denver during the fifties, Ralph _____ .

23. Colorado's hitting coach who blasted 414 homers during his long major league career, Darrell _____ .

24. Infielder drafted by the Rockies from the Reds' organization, Freddie _____ .

DOWN

1. Reliever drafted from the Milwaukee Brewers, Darren_____ .

2. The Rockies drafted this infielder from the Red Sox, then shipped him off to the Dodgers, Jody_____ .

3. Former Expos' pitching coach, he now holds the same position for the Rockies, Larry_____ .

4. The Rockies' top farm team plays in nearby Colorado_____ .

6. Left-handed pitcher drafted from the Detroit Tigers, Scott _____ .

7. Former Blue Jay infielder signed by the Rockies, Nelson_____ .

10. This long-time AL manager got his first managing assignment in Denver in 1968, Billy_____ .

11. Power hitting catcher drafted from the Bosox, _____ .

12. The Denver Triple-A team changed their name to the_____ in 1985.

15. Catching prospect drafted from the Yankees' roster, Brad_____ .

16. Home ballpark of the Rockies, Mile _____ Stadium.

17. The Rockies second pick in the expansion draft, Yankee third baseman Charlie_____ .

19. Before he became the symbol of the "Amazing Mets," he belted 42 homers for Denver in 1956, _____ Thorneberry.

FLORIDA MARLINS

Solution on page 145.

ACROSS

5. Hard-throwing right-hander drafted from the Astros, he posted a 6-4 record for Houston in 1991, Ryan _____ .

8. Home ballpark of the Marlins, Joe _____ Stadium.

9. Marlins' GM, Dave_____ .

10. Florida is known as the_____ State.

11. National League All-Star catcher as a Padre in 1989, Benito_____ .

12. Third base coach for the Marlins, Cookie_____ .

15. Outfielder chosen from the Yankees in the expansion draft, native Floridian Carl_____ .

16. 1992 Olympic baseball champions.

20. This Hall of Famer pitched for the Triple-A Miami Marlins in the fifties, _____ Paige.

21. Marlins' second baseman, former Expo, Bret _____ .

22. First baseman drafted from the Royals, Jeff_____ .

23. Reliever drafted from the California Angels by the Marlins, Bryan_____ .

DOWN

1. This Marlin hurler was the NL's starter in the 1990 All-Star Game, Jack_____ .

2. Outfielder drafted from the California Angels, Junior_____ .

3. Marlin call-ups will have a long flight from the team's Triple-A affiliate in _____ .

4. Highly regarded pitching prospect drafted from the Mets, Jose_____ .

6. This shortstop played in three World Series with the Oakland A's, Walt___ .

7. The Marlins' number one expansion draft pick, outfielder_____ Wilson.

9. This Florida slugger was Japan's home run champion for three consecutive seasons, Orestes_____ .

13. The Marlins drafted this veteran pitcher from the Pirates, then dealt him to the Phillies, Danny_____ .

14. Catcher drafted from the San Francisco Giants, Steve _____ .

17. Louisville Slugger.

18. Former Met infielder signed by the Marlins, _____ Magadan.

19. The Marlins drafted pitching prospect Trevor Hoffman from the roster of this team.

SOLUTIONS

Baltimore Orioles

```
S   I S L E R       B U M B R Y       S H E L B Y
T   I           P       L   I       H       A     E
E   E S T R A D A   A   I   L       M C N A L L Y N
P   V           I   I   L L   M C G R E R       M C
H   E     G A R C I A   I   G R   B U F O R D   D O
E L R O D     G E   B E L A N G E R   V       H A N K
N   S     W A T T   R       A N   G     E R   A N   A
S       R A B   T R I   B   S H O C K E R   D   A   L
        R O B I N S O N   O   R   R I C H A R D S
      H   W A       D   D     P   K   W A L L
    D O B S O N   W I L L I A M S     A L   A   B
    O   I L   K Y   O   C   K   L     M   C   A   R
    B O O G   S     S   K   I   M   W E A V E R A
    G O L S O N       E T C H E B A R R E N     D Y
          D A U E R           R                 Y
```

Boston Red Sox

```
H       W           T     P I L G R I M S
C O L L I N S       T I A N T       O   N     D O M
  O     S       B A M B I N O       O   S   D O Y L E
S P A C E M A N     B   U       R   B   T   O Y L   P
B R U N A N S K Y       U R L   O R   I C L E M E N S
E   N   I   B       R E G G I E   R   E   N       S K
M   G O O D M A N   S O     M A Y S     R E M Y     Y
E   L I   Q U I N T A N A   S T     S A S K Y     F
L   I A   U       A R M   A G G A N I S   Y     E N
P E N A   R E D       M             T   L       N W A
A   R I C O   T   C A M P B E L L   E   Y       A Y
N   E L       T U   S   O     B O G G S         Y
E L   S P L E N D I D   R     E     Y A W K E Y
L Y N N   B A R R E T T   S T A P L E T O N
```

136

Cleveland Indians

```
    L       B           S P E A K E R       W A H O O
B O U D R E A U         A               R       A   D
  P       A     V       P   S T I E B   S C O R E
  E       V     E       T       L E N B A R K E R
A Z C U E   R     S K I N N E R   A   S   T   E R
L O M A R   S K I N N E R   A   S   T   E R
  A   C   D O W E L L         J O H N     F R A N C O
M C D O W E L L             J O H N     F R A N C O
A R I O L I N   C O V E L E S K I   D E L A Y
R       O L I N   C O V E L E S K I   D E L A Y
        T   B E L L E   L     B     E     D O B Y
A V I L A   O F     B E R N A Z A R D       O     Y
A N   D   A   F         R       E R         N
D R   C   B U T L E R       B   E R   K E L T N E R
R O C K Y   Y     O N         R G         L       A
E             O N   G A R C I A     L E A G U E
```

Detroit Tigers

```
    N       R O W E       K A L I N E       H       G
K E L L     H           E M     A R Y   J   I L     R E
  W       N   I     B   M   R O N L E F L O R E   E
H O   N O R T H R U P   P   Y       N L           N B
O     L   A     O N     G A T     H E N N E M A N   B
G U L L I C K S O N     A T E     O     I   R       E R
S       C   E   K     B O O N E   N     T E         B
E       K   R   E         T     G S     D E E R     G
R   T       R   N E W S O M       S     T T
L   B R I D G E S       I L       T       M     T T L E
E   R O           E L   T         D O Y L E   L E
M C A U L I F F E     C U Y L E R   T O       E T     P A D R E
O   T       R Y     A R L   C     O   C R A W F O R D
N     C   Y     A R L   C   O               N       R E
  T R A M M E L L       B       C R A W F O R D     N
    S   A           G I B S O N   O             N     R E
F R E E H A N               T       B R I G G S
```

Milwaukee Brewers

```
    L I S T A C H       P L E S A C       M
B       R       I   H   H I     V E       S C O T T
R   C   E     O G L I V I E     V         L   I
A   E   B     U     S     L   V U C K O V I T C H
B I C H E T T E     L E     C     M   U   T O
E   I   H       R A     W A L L B A N G E R S
N   L   O     S   G     E     B   R O       S A N D E R S
D   C A R D I N A L S   S     B O R N   Y O U N T   T
E R       N   M       N T       R I C K Y     N   D
  H   H       T     W E S           K         B E E R S
N A V A R R O   N I E V E S       S E L I G   F     B
A A   H     N     R         W       S         F     O
S   R P E     S     C     M O N E Y   T H O M A S   S I
H E N R Y   W A L T O N       S C H U L T Z       O
```

New York Yankees

```
            P                       B E R R A           M E L I D O
    M I L I T E L L O               O                   I Z E     Y L E         I T
L         P             A           U         L O P E Z         L E             T M
A         P   R I Z Z U T O             F E       I N E           B             M A R
R         A             Z           O N E R         I N E     G U I D R Y
S T E I N B R E N N E R                   R U T H         B     K     D I M     A R Y
E         D O W N I N G                   A     R         K     D I M A
N         O L               O             G     R                 P A G E
K E       P R     S K O W R O N           G               C       A G G
R A S C H I               E             M E               H       G G
A       N A     C H A S E         L I N Z             H A W K I N S
D E N T   K               L I N Z           K N         D           O
        F         F           S           U D           C H
H A M I L T O N     T A R T A B U L L           E           I R O N
        S         R           O           E L           E             N G
R I C H A R D S O N       S E L K I R K                           G
```

Toronto Blue Jays

```
          C       S       G       C       W H I T E         J E S S E
      C A R T E R         U     O   N         A           C             S
          N       O       N     T A B L E R       G R I F F I N         E A
          D       T       S     B                     I                 A G
  W H I T T       L       T         R             B       O L E R U D   U D
          O       L       R         S             B       X             L L
          S T I E B       M U L L I N I K S       A       H             L L
          T       M       E             E         L       I
          J I M Y         L             L         O       B             L
              R           A   B O R D E R S           F I L E R         E R
  M A N U E L L E E                                   T     I         M A
  C               L                                 F     D         N     N
  G U Z M A N     F L A N A G A N         J O H N                   C
  R               I                       A             I         O       C
  I       H E N K E             L I R I A N O           M                 Z
  F       G                               L     S       O                 Y
  F       W E L L S         K E Y         O         B L A C K             K
```

California Angels

```
  C                       G         H             W               L
  A B B O T T     T     B R E W E R S         R E I C H A R D T
  R         O S         T H     R I C H     Z     H N         F R E G O S I
  E         T       F O R S C H         Z A H N       I N             G
  W I T T           O M A S         R         O       F         S
          M C C A S K I L L           A N A H E I M   L       B O O N E   D
          K           A S         G N E               D             N     E C
  R         A         S           G         P         R               N   C
  M O O R E           S           N E       P     P   B L Y L E V E N     I
  J             B A Y L O R       E       L O R   E       Y         R     N
  D A D D Y     U         T           R   L O     S A L M O N     G E N E S
  A             G         R                       A           T A N A N A H
  S             E         R   K N O O P           R       B O N     R
  H A R V E Y       S         C H A N C E         N             N   F E L I X
```

Chicago White Sox

```
S                     W               G       G A N D I           L
B O     D E B U S S C H E R E         L                           U
S O             H             A       M                   F E R N A N D E Z     Z
L A N D I S       A V         M       A     S   O             P P     L Y O N S     I
              L A W   P E T E R S     S     O   N             P       I           N   S
A L T R O C K         M               O             S     N           K           K         I
A       S             A P A R I C I O               T H I G P E N
N       R                 N O         K             O           R
C O M I S K E Y         O             R             S E A V E R
E       C D           O V             S             L           E N
        C D             T H O M A S               E           N
W O O D         I                     V       A     S           T           H
        W       C I C O T T E         C       L     S           U           O
P I E R C E             R             C O L I S E U M           R     F O X
                R       T             E       E                 U     U
        L A R U S S A         W Y N N         W A L S H               G H
```

Kansas City Royals

```
W             P                   J O Y N E R       R         G           M
M A C F A R L A N E               E                 O         O R D Y     O N A R C H S
      H       T           I       F       M A Y B E R R Y     D           A
      H A N E Y           K       E V E N     M O N T G O M E R Y         R
      A N         K             N S       R       G         S O N         E
H       C O W E N S             R       G             O             N
E A L       Q             B       L E I B R A N D T           E I               C H S
A       S T       U       A       S       M C R A E     O           S           F
L Y       H       M I L L E R       Z       P         R T E R       E N         A R
B       U M A R K         B         B       A         P O R T E R A             I
U S     M       P         O         R       I             A             R       C
S B I R D     Q U I S E N B E R R Y         T           E               H       G U R A
Y       T             L             A T H L E T I C S
```

Minnesota Twins

```
V                 V       Y O S T         K A A T             C
K I L L E B R E W         L       R I C E       A G             A R D I N A L S
O             R       R       L I V         A     L A U D N E R   C
B L U E J A Y S       R       I V           A I N E     L Y     I L     K       D
A       M E L E       S       G A G N E             V E R N O N         I
      T   O     R     P   E   L O S T       S M               R A       N
      A   R     P A G L I A N O S K I N   B A T T E Y                   A L S
P E R R A N O S K I           D           L A         L A N D R E A U X     C
N       I       G           R T           O   H E R B Y       M I N C H E R     R O
      S C H A T Z E D E R       G   B E         B             E           N I
S T P A U L             E       R   B     B O   K O O S M A N           I
M E T R O     W E S T           R   K I R B Y               L A R K I N
```

Oakland Athletics

```
W   E L CH         B           C     C O C H R A N E
W I L     A R         W A D D E L L       O       L A   A
L I N D B L A D     O   L A U   H O L T Z M A N   R
I           I   N     S     C     P E N N A N T     E D A   S
A M C C A T T Y   A N       B L U E     D     S   B A     H
S   Z       L S   E W A R     E     R     M     E N   R U
  C R A M E R   T     H O M E R U N     N O R R I S
  N     I   C   G     T       O             R         D
  B I N G     W           O             N O F
  A     L       C   F O S S E   S I M M O N S
  R             E   R                 U L
  R         G R O V E                 L
  P O W E R   V         C A M P A N E R I S
```

Seattle Mariners

```
      K I N G D O M E             S C H O O L E R
  D       U       O               O                 R
  A   F   N   B O O N E   M A R T I N E Z       E
  V A L L E   Z         R         T             Y
  I   E M     Z   P R E S L E Y   N I N T E N D O   N
  S   I N G         M   P         E     B R A U N   O
      G   W I L L I A M S         R     B         R L
          H   D E L U C I A       H     B       R A   D
      V   A   A R G Y R O S   R O M O   T   S W A N   S
      I Z I S K   O     Y     T   B     T I E   L   B
      Q   O     B     A N   S   B E A T T I E   Y   U
      U   N     E         R U P P E R T   C U T T O   H
      E       R U P P E R T       U   T     O W E N N
      C L E M E N S   B A N N I S T E R             R
```

Texas Rangers

```
        J     S T A U B           J           R
      E U   S I E         R O D R I G U E Z     O
      P A L M E R         B R I       U   K     G
      S   I   R R     G O N Z A L E Z M     L I N   E
      T   O   R A     G   N K M     U Z     K         R
    T E D       A     R I E M A     M A     I N   C   S
      I     D O N O V A N     L     A N   S   O R F K
      N     B       E         I     C     C   R R   E
    H O W A R D           S T E N H O U S E   E A   S
    A     R I   C       V   O       C     A       U
    R U S S E L L   K E R N   M     R R   M A R T I N   N D
    R     A M   L Y D       N     C L   A   R         B
    A     P A L M E I R O       V A L E N T I N   E
    H     L         N           I     S   I         R
    B U E C H E L E     R Y A N       N               G
```

Chicago Cubs

```
G R A C E       E           J               L I G H T S       T           D           K
O               L       J O D Y       M               A R T   S T A N   T I N K E R   D U R O C H E R   K E S S
M O R E L A N D         Y           D U N S T O N     N       E                       O               I
T               W                   D                 T                               R               N
W   I P P O             R E U S C H E L               L       A R C H E R             E
H       A   T   C               X                     T       S               T       H       E
A       S U T T E R     R               W E S T       T       S U T           T H R E E       R
L       S   H   E Y                                   A   C                   H   A           R
E       E       C           A S S E N M A C H E R             L               K
S       A       L       C               A N S O N             I               E       B
R E U L B A C H         A N             S             N       F   F R E Y     O W A N
I       A       K E N   H U B B S                             F                       N
G       A N T S     S   C                               G L E N N   N         L A W
S               D   O       E V E R S                     E                   E       G
    I V Y       N           G                           E   H E R M A N               N
```

Montreal Expos

```
Y               B R O O K S       F       C       V A L A N G E
O W E N     D   W                     O C   O R A N G E
U           P A D R E S               C           L       R
M O N D A Y P           N       S A N T O V E N I   R I S S O
A       L   M       R A Y             N       F   T       O       R
N   J   A   M C G A F F I G A N       G       I   I       O       A
S   A   R   E   R       Y   A L       G     S T O N E M A N       I
C A R L     W E T T E L A N D         R O S         E       N
R   R               S       R                 R O S         C L   E
O L Y M P I C       H       R O D G E R S             T C   S
M   A               I       A                         L A   L
A   R   B A R B E R I E     G   M A R S H A L L       A
R   A               L E A     M A C             I
T   S   O L I V E R D       G A R D N E R             R
I               H I L L     B U R K E     C A R T E R
E
```

New York Mets

```
I N N I S     L E A C H         O     K A N E H L
      H               I         J           O O
M A C K E Y   F   S E A V E R   D   H O J O   K
C     B   T O R B O R G         A S T R O S       K
R E   O N G     N               R           S     N
Y O U N G   G E N T R Y   E L I O       C R A   I
N     I L         D   R   I   P E C O T A   K E N T
O   C L E N D E N O N       K       F   R   H T
L   A       M   Z   L E S   W O B O D A   A J
D   Z   M O D G E S     S W       T       G O
  G I L H O D G E S     R   G O O D E N   L E H
H   M   M   O   I   R   O               C   O N
U   E   K O O S M A N   T   R E A R D O N   N S
T H R O N E B E R R Y               S W A N   O
```

Philadelphia Phillies

```
        B       K R U K           M               B O W A
        B U L L   O           O Z A R K           P     A I
    P   N     E   B       O R I       D     D E L A H A N T K
    U   N   F R E G O S I   O   O     D E N             I   U
    D   I   E R   N     O L E   X A N D E R     P A R R I S   S
    D E N N Y   T S     L E S       R O Y A L S H         H
    I           M     U N S E R       O       E         O R T
    H E A T   U N S E R     C A S H     M   S C H M I D T
    A       A Y   H     A       E   S C H M I D   S I   R
    D A U L T O N   A S A M     W       G       E L I   A M
            O R     H     G     I S E   R A W     E R     A R
        T   H     L L     B E D R O S I A N         R     A O
        H       A   U   R   O S
    H O L L A N D   D   E N N I S             T R I L L O
        N           D
```

Pittsburgh Pirates

```
    B U R G E S S       T         M E N D O Z A
    E   A     S   T   P A R K E R   J   A       Z A N E
    L   I N D   T U     A     R   J I M L E Y L A N E D
    I   D   V A N S L Y K E   I L L E Y   A E
    N   Y   M   S T   N     A   L E         M O O S E
    D   A   M U R T   A R   O   D A C Y         O N     S
    A L O U   R   T     G E   V I M       W A G N E R   E R
        D   T H R E E   G I U S T I       A L       N E T
    M O T A U   I   L   N C H     T E K U L V E       T T
    C   U G   E N     E         F       F M E
    Y   R H O D E N   C A R E Y   R O O K E R       F
    L   H E A T O N     N E       M   L     N T     A
    E   A       T T         H A D D I X   T         C
    R A L P H   T         R         N   V E A L E
```

St. Louis Cardinals

```
        M       H   H   S     H O R N S B Y       M
    G A R A G I O L A   F   S L E E     R     U S C D
        X       E R   A     U R     H O U S E     A
        J A V I E R N   E   Y O G I   B R E C H E E N I
    P H I L L I E S   R     G   H   H       O O   Z Z I E L
    E       L   R   G     S T R E E T   O   P     I
    P A G N O Z Z I     B R Y N   W     E   R E D   F
    E       Y     B     O   N     A   K             L
    R E A G A N   S O   H A I N E S   B R O G L I O O
            L         O       D       U R     E O   D
        B   S H A N N O N     E       Z   J   O     D
    B O T T O M L E Y   M       C Y Y O U N G S
        C   I   U       A
        K   M U S I A L   D I Z Z Y D E A N
```

Atlanta Braves

```
M         H     J U S T I C E             B R E A M     M
F U L T O N   O N       A     G A R R     B U R D       E
S   P A H N E     T W I N S     A R L     C A R T Y     S
  P   H     N E     A I N         L     Y A N K E E S   S
  H   Y     C R A N D A L L             D     E         E
  F         C H A M       D A L L   C     M   M A T H E W S
  U         B A N C R O F T     L   O   N       E V A N S M
  C         M     B   L     S   C   J O H N S O N   M A N I
  H       S M O L T Z     O   C O   N T I L L   I N D I A N S T
    M O R T O N     S     N I X O N   I L L   A V E R Y   A H
    O   R   S   S   E     N     G     L     B E R G E   A R
    R   T   S   V     C A B R E R A   A   U   R Y     O N T
    O       O   E R O         R       B E R U H     G A N T
    N I E K R O           M A R A N V I L L E
```

Cincinnati Reds

```
      V         B E N C H         D       P       O
    L A R K I N     U         C O N C E P C I O   N E I L L
  E   D   L   A     X       A R D   E   R   I N   I   L
  P   E   U   S   O   H A R R I S   S W I N D E L L   L
  A   R E Z   Y   G L O V E   D     N     N   E L L   L
      B R O W N I N G   J   A   N   L E G S   L A B O
      E   S     O     R O U S H   E         R   S A B O
  B L A C K W E L L     S E R   L O M B A R D   I P
    C   I     A   S A N D E R S   L M       K Y   P
  D E R O N   M     D A   I     A L O N E         V A
    R   R       R O N I M O   M C N A M A R A   D A
        G E R O N I S                 O N E Y
  F R O N T   E       C R O S L E Y           M A Y
```

Houston Astros

```
      R           C     T U R F       K
    B A G W E L L   C A B E L L     F O     K I L E
  M A Y     I L         D E N     F A R R E L L   E
  A T   O S U N A     B   K E N       N S C   C R U D
  E M   O   O T     V I R D O N   R I C H A R D   R U Z
  C A M I N I T I   B I G G       Y   E     K     G O
  A L   X A V I E R   G I   D I E R K E R   N     O P
  L A       B A R T   H O W E     L D   R   H E E P   D A
  A S       A R T     L     E S H   I N   F     P     V I
  S O N N Y   I N C A V I G L I A   N     P     D A V I S
  H B       P H I L L I E S   W A L K E R     E
  B Y     H A R N I S C H   F O R T Y F I V E S
```

Los Angeles Dodgers

```
          R A V I N E             R U S S E L L         M O T A
          A             S         E               R       A         L
C A M I L L I     S U   E         R O S E B O R O         S
O X   N   N O H I T T E R               K   I N E             T
    A   Z       O                 V A N C E     A R         O
    M   U       N                 Y           E     B         N
P O D R E S   L     E                   C       S N I D E R   R
    R   L A S O R D A     J A Y       Y         E             A
K O U F A X     P         G         M           O W E N       N
    S   U       R E I S E R           P         C             C
H     R   W       S         R     K A R R O S         R A U   A
O     I   H             M         W     N             M
O M A L L E Y       M O       I   E               B       S
T     L   A             O R E L     L     L           E B B E T S
O     O S T E E N                 L     L             S T A
N                       S H A R P E R S O N
```

San Diego Padres

```
              R         T E U F E L       R         T I G E R     R
G O S S A G E           E               R           W             I
A     H       N         R       M C C O V E Y       Y             D
R     O W     D A V I S N                           N             D
V     W       Y         A     L                   E N Z           O
E             Y         N     I E K R O                           C
Y     S H E F F I E L D       D     F             T               H
    S   I             M       E     F         G O M E Z
G A S T O N           E T Z G E R             T
    N   S             S       H U R S T       E M P
    T   O                     R         M U R P H Y
    I   N                     S     K E N N E D Y
    A             S T R O M         M         T
    G             I       M         E         O
C O L B E R T     T O     O     N E T T L E S
                  O       N           B E N E S
```

San Francisco Giants

```
          D A V E N P O R T         R H O D E S     O T T
          A         O               A         W     D E L L
M I T C H E L L     O         L     R     M I L L E R
A         O         O     B R Y A N T       N         L         H
R         N         D             C         H I G H   L         E
I         E     M A T H E W S O N           H         L         R
C         L     A   R         S     T     W I L H E L M         M
H A L I C K I   T   I         S     R A T L E E       V         A
A         I     H   V       S A L   I     I           N         N
L             M C R A I G     U     V     A           S         W
W H I T E Y   G     N   M     E S N A H A N           M         A
H E A R T     R     A   E     R I           S A N F O R D       R
I             A     H U B B E L L           O         R         D
T           S W I F T   S     A             L A V E L L E
E             C A N D L E S T I C K                   D
Y
```

Colorado Rockies

```
H E N R Y       B E A R S       B A Y L O R
O           E           E             L       I
L     G E B H A R D       P R I N G S   R A   D R   I
E         D     M A R N       E R I C         E     A N O     Z
S       G A L A R R A G A                 D A N T E     Z
H     A U   R   A R       R               E         P
H I G   S M I T H   T       M           H A S H B Y
I G     M     I N           H A S S E Y   A       Y     R
H O U   K               M A R       Y   E V A N S
              B E N A V I D E S
```

Florida Marlins

```
A           F           E       M       B O W E N     N
R O B B I E   E       D O M B R O W S K I   E       I
M           L     D E M O N T O N   A R           S   G
S U N S H I N E   E           T       I A G O     S   E
T         X     S A N T I A G O       N       D         L
R O J A S       T           E V E R E T T
O     A C U B A   R       N       Z       D
N     K A     A   A     D             C     K       R E D S
G     S A T C H E L           B A R B E R I
      O                   D A V
C O N I N E       H A R V E Y
```

BATTER UP WITH MASTERS PRESS!

You Can Teach Hitting

Dusty Baker, Marv Bittinger, and Jeff Mercer

More than a set of instructions and guidelines for swinging your bat, *You Can Teach Hitting* takes you from seleting your bat to selecting your pitch. Lavishly illustrated with full color photographs and stunning computer graphics throughout, *You Can Teach Hitting* is truly a unique book!

```
256 pages • 8½ × 9½
0-940279-73-8 • $24.95
color photos throughout
paper
```

Spalding Baseball Drill Book

Gordon Gillespie

A practical handbook for coaches at all levels of play interested in improving both individual and team performance. Contains activities designed to keep players at every level of competition busy and motivated during practice.

```
224 pages • 7 × 10
0-940279-59-2 • $14.95
b/w photos
paper
```

Beisbol: Latin Americans and the Grand Old Game

Michael M. Oleksak and Mary Adams Oleksak

Major league rosters of the 1990's include names such as Rijo, Canseco, Fernandez, and Tartabull. *Beisbol* explains how the greats from "south of the border" broke down cultural, racial, and linguistic barriers to survive and thrive in Major League Baseball.

```
320 pages • 6 × 9
0-940279-35-5 • $22.95
photo insert
cloth
```

Between the Lines: One Athlete's Struggle to Escape the Nightmare of Addiction

Steve Howe with Jim Greenfield

In 1983, Steve Howe was the premier relief pitcher in the National League and the toast of the Los Angeles Dodgers. Young, rich, and famous, he had everything - until a cocaine addiction nearly destroyed his life. Howe's story, including his struggle to reclaim his self-esteem, is one of courage and inspiration.

```
288 pages • 6 × 9
0-940279-25-8 • $17.95
photo insert
cloth
```

Masters Press books are available from bookstores or by calling (800) 722-2677.

MASTERS PRESS

DEAR VALUED CUSTOMER,

Masters Press is dedicated to bringing you timely and authoritative books for your personal and professional library. As a leading publisher of sports and fitness books, our goal is to provide you with easily accessible information on topics that interest you written by the most qualified authors. You can assist us in this endeavor by checking the box next to your particular areas of interest.

We appreciate your comments and will use the information to provide you with an expanded and more comprehensive selection of titles.

Thank you very much for taking the time to provide us with this helpful information.

Cordially,
Masters Press

Areas of interest in which you'd like to see Masters Press publish books:

☐ COACHING BOOKS
   Which sports? What level of competition?

☐ INSTRUCTIONAL/DRILL BOOKS
   Which sports? What level of competition?

☐ FITNESS/EXERCISE BOOKS
   ☐ Strength—Weight Training
   ☐ Body Building
   ☐ Other

☐ REFERENCE BOOKS
   what kinds?

☐ BOOKS ON OTHER
   Games, Hobbies
   or Activities

Are you more likely to read a book or watch a video-tape to get the sports information you are looking for?

I'm interested in the following sports as a participant:

I'm interested in the following sports as an observer:

Please feel free to offer any comments or suggestions to help us shape our publishing plan for the future.

Name _____ Age _____

Address _____

City _____ State _____ Zip _____

Daytime phone number _____

BUSINESS REPLY MAIL

FIRST CLASS MAIL   PERMIT NO. 1317   INDIANAPOLIS IN

POSTAGE WILL BE PAID BY ADDRESSEE

MASTERS PRESS

2647 WATERFRONT PKY EAST DR DEPT WF
INDIANAPOLIS IN 46209-1418